Trees

Francesca Greenoak

Macdonald Educational

Editor Kate Woodhouse
Assistant Editor Caroline Russum
Design and Picture Research Ikon
Production Philip Hughes

First published 1976

Macdonald Educational Ltd.
Holywell House
Worship Street
London EC2A 2EN

contents

ISBN 0 356 05287 7

What is a tree?

Plants with a difference

Although their size and magnificence make trees distinctly recognizable, they are not a separate category of plants. A tree is simply a plant with a woody stem. On the face of it this is not exactly an exciting or informative definition. But it opens the door to some surprises: the nettle for instance is a relative of the elm, the hollyhock of the lime (or linden) tree.

Trees and people

Defining what trees mean, not just to botanists but to people as a whole, is more difficult. There is scarcely any aspect of human history which has not some kind of link with trees, whether it be pleasure, war, food, art or architecture. The story of trees is a long and continuing one. Some of the first farming implements, domestic utensils and houses were made of wood. We need only to glance around us to see how much trees and wood are still part of our everyday lives. The book you are reading now was once a growing tree!

▶ Not much bigger than your hand, but unmistakably a tree. The art of raising these miniatures, or *bonsai*, comes from Japan, where huge value is set by them.

▶ The "duck's foot" shape of its leaf makes the ginkgo immediately recognizable. The leaf looks just the same where it grows today as it does in the ancient fossils.

Today we can buy almost any item we want from the shops, but in times past people used what was at hand to make the things they needed such as food, medicine and tools.

◀ The elder has a vast store of uses. Young branches have a pithy centre which is removed easily to make pipes, whistles or pea shooters! Older wood is carved into skewers, pegs or toys. There are three elder dyes: green from the leaves, black from the bark and purple from the berries. Bruised leaves act as a fly repellent.

Tasty jams and wines can be made from both berries and flowers. Elder was known as "the countryman's medicine chest" and some of the cures are still used. Try some of the old usages yourself.

▶ Coconut palms too provide a public service. The nut gives food and drink and its husk is made into mats, rope and baskets. Trunks provide building, and leaves thatching material. Coconut oil is used in soap and margarine.

The trees of prehistory

The age of plants

Long ago before people lived on the earth, plants grew in abundance. It had to be that way. In order to live animals (and humans too are animals) need to eat plants or creatures that themselves feed off plants. The first plants were simple one-celled structures. Trees, although much more complex, also have a long history. The giant horsetails and tree mosses of prehistoric times no longer survive but their relatives are still living in a much smaller form.

The origins of coal

For millions of years, giant horsetails, ferns and mosses dominated the landscape. It is these plants we have to thank for our coal deposits. Coal is the remains of vast quantities of these ancient trees.

From trees to coal

There is carbon in all plants and there were large amounts contained in early forests. Prehistoric forests were swampy places and countless numbers of trees died and fell, and were changed over millions of years through the forces of heat and pressure, into another form of carbon—coal.

A lone survivor

There is one remarkable prehistoric tree, the ginkgo, still growing. Fossil evidence shows that this tree grew as long as 250 million years ago, yet you are quite likely to see it thriving in parks or town streets today, despite dirt and pollution. Generally speaking though we can only find out about prehistoric trees from pollen and fossil remains.

▼ The chart below indicates the evolution of plant and animal life from earliest times. The chart has been built up in the light of fossil evidence. The green lines vary in width to give a general idea of how the plant populations fluctuated. The pictures on the right illustrate some present-day representatives of the range of plant life.

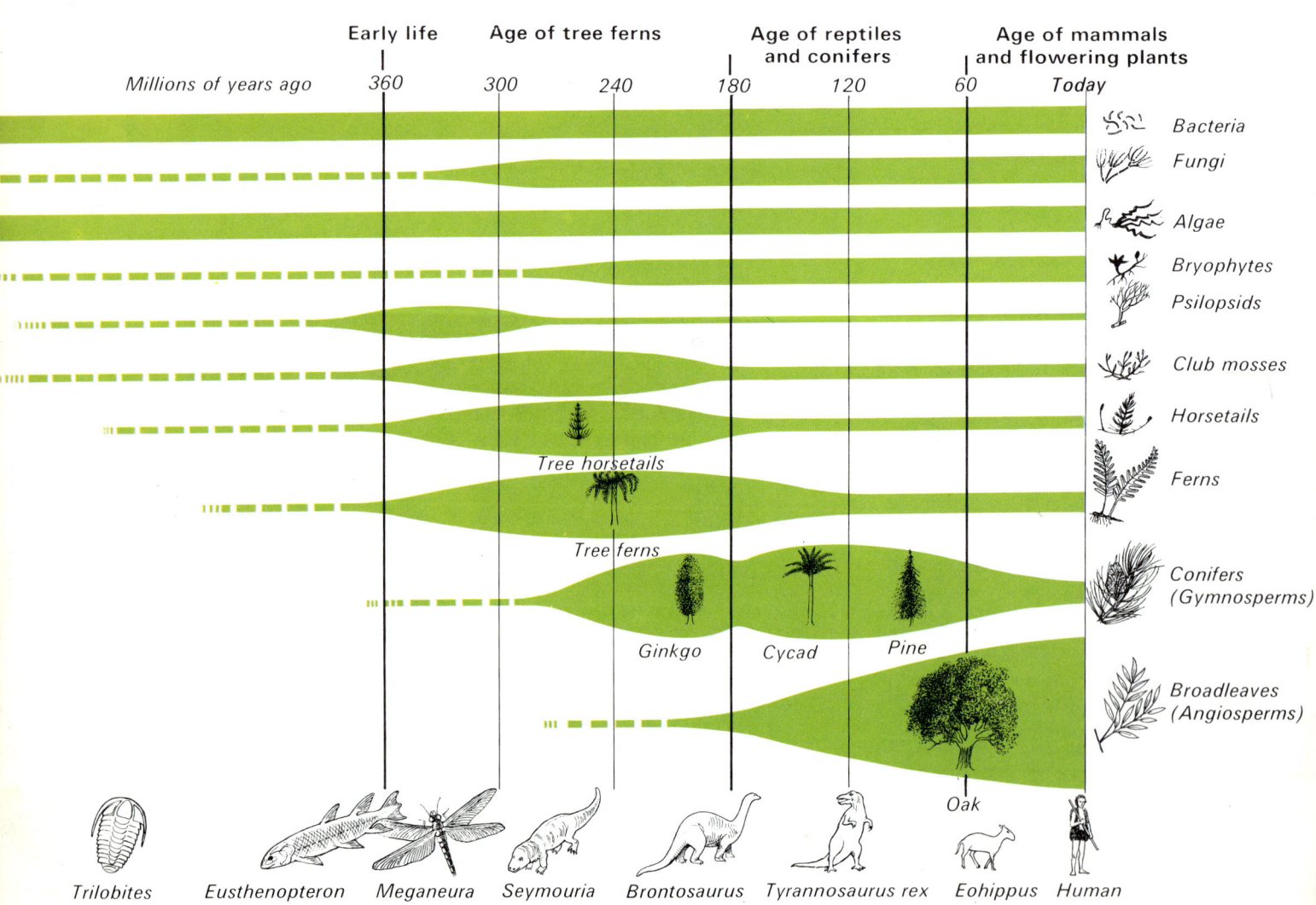

The three different groups of trees

Seed

Leaf

Cone *Seed* *Needle*

Date with seed inside

Leaf

Scots pine
Conifers are mainly fast growing evergreens with tall straight trunks and needle-like leaves. They bear their seeds on cones and when small, the seedlings have a number of early leaves or cotyledons. The rich warm smell of pinewoods comes from a sticky substance called resin.

Oak
Broadleaves are also known as flowering trees. Their seeds have a protective case (or ovary) round them. In cool climates many broadleaves are deciduous, that is they shed their broad leaves in autumn and the trees remain dormant throughout the winter. The seedlings have two cotyledons.

Date palm
Palms are of great importance in tropical regions, providing food and shelter. Palm trees have no annual rings; their trunks are like giant stalks, with "bundles" of woody tissue running up them. The unbranched trunk is topped by a cluster of huge leaves, some of them up to 4.5 metres long.

▲ A petrified forest is literally a forest turned to stone. The natural tissues of the wood are replaced by stone. A petrified tree can be a perfect reproduction not only of outward shape, but of the internal structure of the wood, right down to individual cells.

► This perfectly-preserved poplar leaf is in fact about 27 million years old. Its shape and structure are exactly reproduced in the stone. Fossil remains like this, found in rock and coal, give us much of the evidence we need to piece together the history of trees.

Conifers evergreen softwoods

Conifer foliage

White pine

Cypress

Silver fir

Dawn redwood

Larch

Norway spruce

▲ All conifer foliage seems very similar at first glance, but look more closely at this selection. **White pine** has long needles in clusters of five (most other pine needles are in twos and threes) bound in a sheath. **Cypress** has leaves overlapping all around the twig in a scaly cord. **Silver fir** has individual flat soft leaves with notches in the ends. **Dawn redwood** has flat leaves ranged in opposite ranks along the twig. **Larch** has leaves in **rosettes** on woody pegs. **Norway spruce,** our Christmas tree, has four-sided prickly leaves growing on tiny individual pegs which leave the twigs rough when they drop off.

The retreat to cooler regions

Although conifers are a familiar sight nowadays, there are relatively few compared to the numbers that dominated the prehistoric forests. Very gradually the world's climate changed, becoming warmer and dryer. Broadleaved trees took over as the dominant type of tree and many conifers retreated to less fertile, cooler regions; others died out altogether.

A growing fossil

As recently as 1941, a Chinese botanist came across a dawn redwood (up till then known only as a fossil) growing in a forest in Szechwan, China. At first nobody could believe the news, but other scientists travelled out there and confirmed the discovery. Seeds were collected and now this once-rare tree grows in many places all over the world.

Timber

Much of the coniferous forest we see today is the result of planting by humans. The care and protection given to the trees is amply rewarded. They grow quickly and their wood (known as "softwood") is well suited for many purposes. Papermaking is perhaps the most important. Wood products range from wooden spoons and furniture to door and window frames in the house, from farm fencing and boxes for packing to props for supporting mine shafts.

We can no longer afford to squander our tree resources. Within living memory it was normal for as little as 25% of a tree to be used and the rest wasted. In the face of shortage, we have learned to be more economical. Wood chippings, sawdust and even bark are used in the manufacture of chipboard, packing and fertilizers. Nowadays about 75% of a tree can be used by a good saw mill.

▲ Tall straight trees used to be in great demand for ships' masts.

Conifer shapes

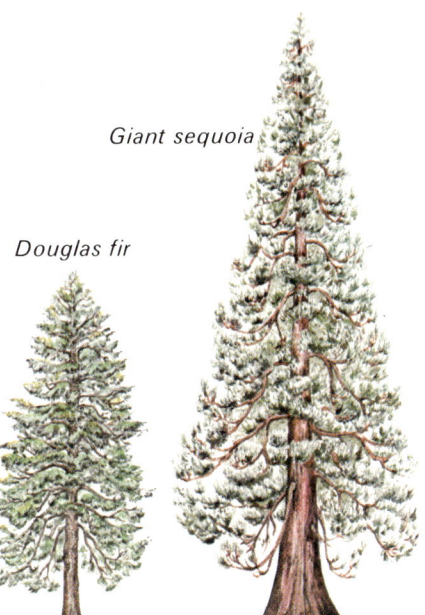

Giant sequoia

Douglas fir

Cedar of Lebanon

Larch

Lawson cypress

▲ Juniper berries are really fleshy cone scales fused together. They take two years to ripen and are used to give gin its flavour.

▼ The thick-skinned seed of the yew is contained in a juicy red cup. The berry is relished by birds, who excrete the poisonous seed before it can harm them.

▲ **Cedar of Lebanon** has a spreading, flat table of branches. **Larch**, one of the few deciduous conifers, is delicately formed with shoots hanging down in soft "caterpillars". **Cypress** is a close-growing pillar shape. **Douglas fir** is a regular conical shape with a slender central stem. **Giant sequoia** is the second tallest and most massive tree in the world, growing in the shape of a long triangle.

▼ **Cones** carry the seeds of conifers; different trees bear different kinds of cone. The beautifully symmetrical **cedar** (11) is easy to tell; this one has fragrant resin on it. **Firs** (9) are more untidy and irregular. **Pines** (2, 7, 8, 10) usually take two years to mature. **Cypress** cones (5) are usually small and so, surprisingly, are those of the **giant sequoia** (4). The **larch** cone (3) sits up on the twig, while the **spruce** (6) and **Douglas fir** (1) hang down.

1   2   3   4   5   6

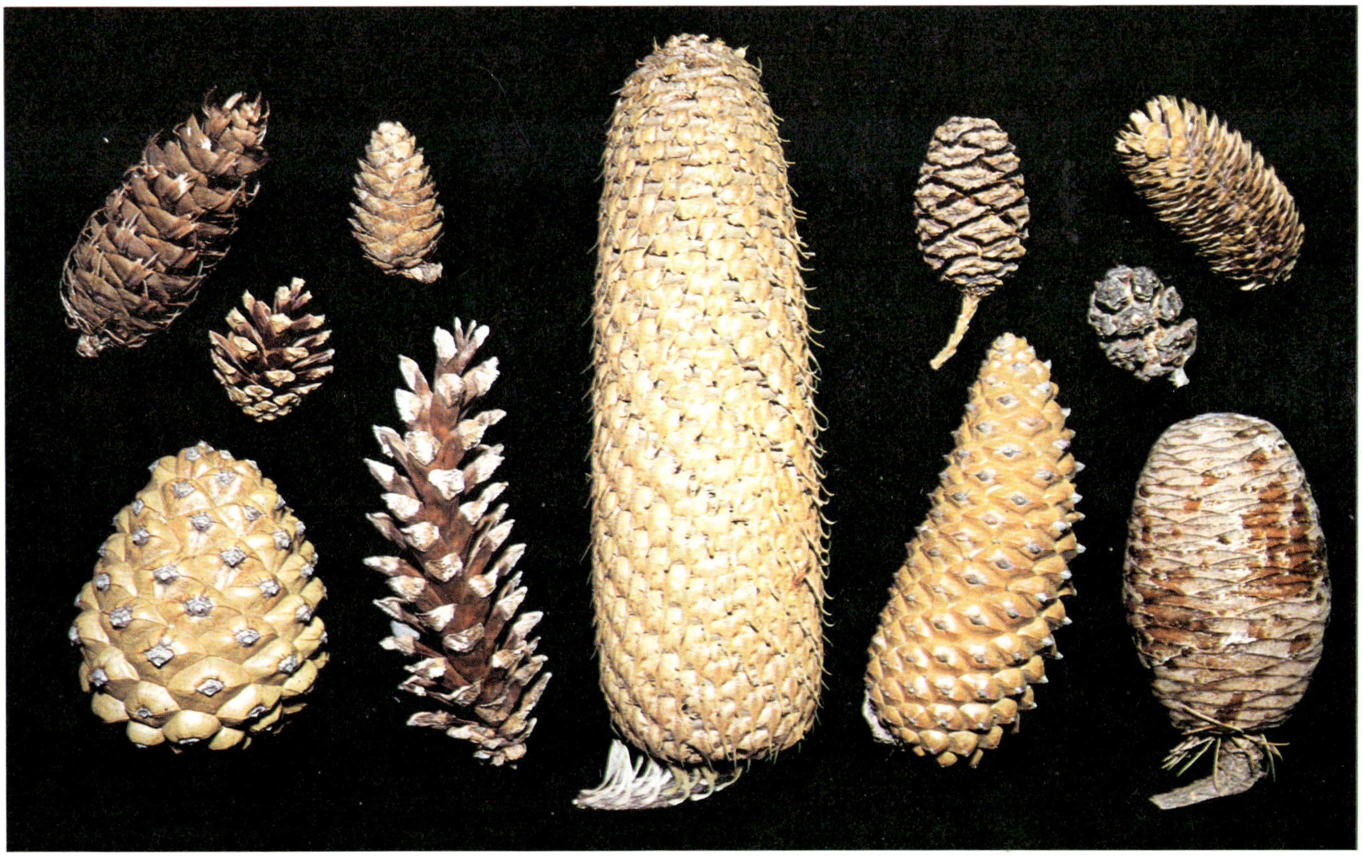

7   8   9   10   11

Broadleaves the dominant hardwoods

Broadleaf foliage

False acacia

Alder

Willow

Holly

Sycamore

Horse chestnut

▲ **False acacia** has delicate pale leaflets. **Alder** has single egg-shaped leaves. **Willow** has long, slender leaves, glossy on the upper side and greyish underneath. The **holly's** glossy evergreen leaves have sharp spines. **Sycamore** has five-lobed leaves. **Horse chestnut** has big leaflets spreading round from the end of the stalk.

The most successful trees

The first broadleaf trees appeared on the landscape at about the time the dinosaurs were dying out. They established themselves so successfully that they are now the most widespread form of trees. Broadleaves all belong to the "dominant" type of plant life of our time, that is, the flowering plants. To give an idea of the variety of broadleaves, there are 49 different broadleaf families, whereas *all* the conifers belong to only six families.

There is no one reason why broadleaved trees were so successful; it was a mixture of several characteristics. Their "broad leaves" catch more of the life-giving sunlight than thin conifer needles. They also have special cells called vessels which give them a better system of taking water up from the soil.

The diversity of broadleaves

Perhaps the most important difference between broadleaves and conifers is that the seeds of broadleaves are encased in an "ovary". This protects the seeds and gives the broadleaves a head start in the race for survival.

People have taken advantage of the diversity of broadleaves for thousands of years. 2,000-year-old wall paintings in Egypt show pomegranates, oranges and figs being cultivated. The modern world takes for granted tree products like rubber, olive oil and beautifully "grained" woods (known as "hardwoods") like oak and ebony, which in the hands of craftsmen make items of furniture and decoration to last for centuries. Some trees like the sumach with its long graceful fronds, are grown simply for their beauty.

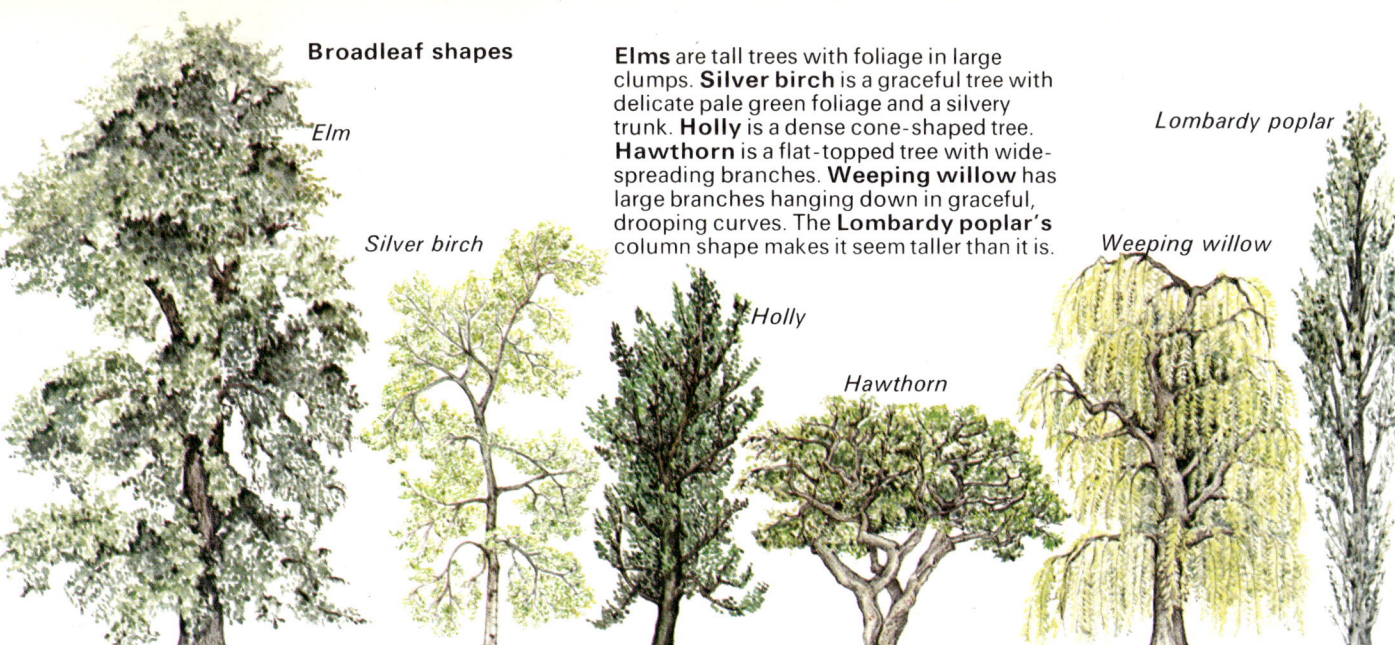

Broadleaf shapes

Elm

Elms are tall trees with foliage in large clumps. **Silver birch** is a graceful tree with delicate pale green foliage and a silvery trunk. **Holly** is a dense cone-shaped tree. **Hawthorn** is a flat-topped tree with wide-spreading branches. **Weeping willow** has large branches hanging down in graceful, drooping curves. The **Lombardy poplar's** column shape makes it seem taller than it is.

Silver birch

Holly

Hawthorn

Lombardy poplar

Weeping willow

▲ Lime wood can take designs of great intricacy. This carving by Grinling Gibbons made three centuries ago still has all its original freshness and vigour.

► The magnificent Octagon tower of Ely Cathedral, England is one of the greatest feats of medieval carpentry and design. Supporting the tower are 16 huge oak timbers.

◄ The floor of this oak wood is covered in bracken. Hazel and bramble grow strongly.

► The earliest printed illustrations were wood cuts. Woodcuts (near right) are made from a block where the wood, usually a soft wood such as pear, is cut with the grain. Using a knife the background is cut away and the lines left in relief to be printed. Wood engraving (far right), a later process dominant in the 19th century, uses the end grain. A hard wood such as boxwood is used and the drawing incised into the wood by a graver (or burin) — a tool like a sharp pointed chisel.

Growing upwards and outwards

Competing for sunlight

At first sight a tree with its woody trunk and its widespread root system below, has little in common with a buttercup, fern, or water-lily. Yet all these plants make the food they need for growth by photosynthesis. All green plants use the chlorophyll in their leaves together with light from the sun to make food from carbon dioxide in the air and water drawn up by the roots from the soil. So the more leaves a plant can expose to sunlight the more food it can make and the better it will thrive.

This is where trees have the advantage. Plants growing low down have to make do with what little sunlight filters through the taller plants, but nothing grows taller than a tree. And trees grow not only upwards but outwards too. In terms of its function, that magnificent structure of trunk and branches is simply something for the tree to hang its leaves upon! A mature oak tree can carry as many as a quarter of a million leaves.

Transporting the food

Once the sugary food or sap has been made in the leaves, it is carried from the leaf veins to the other parts of the tree. The food path goes through the twigs, then down an outer layer of the trunk called the phloem. The food can reach all parts of the tree, the root tips, the cambium in the trunk, the twigs and leaves, along this route.

Air and water

A tree, like a human being, needs to breathe. It takes in oxygen through its leaves and gives out carbon dioxide. The opposite movement of gases happens in photosynthesis. In daylight when plants are photosynthesizing, they give out more oxygen than carbon dioxide.

Plants also give off water through their leaves in quite considerable quantities. It is not known exactly why so much water is transpired. It may be connected with the process of drawing water up from the roots.

The growth of the ash

The flowers of the ash tree come out well before the leaves. The flower in the illustration is a female one from which the ash "key" will later grow. Note how the bud at the tip of the twig is so much larger than the others. The new wood to extend the twig grows from this bud. Leaves alone grow from the other buds. The ash is both wind and insect pollinated.

Leader (twig bud)

Leaf buds

Female flower

Male flowers

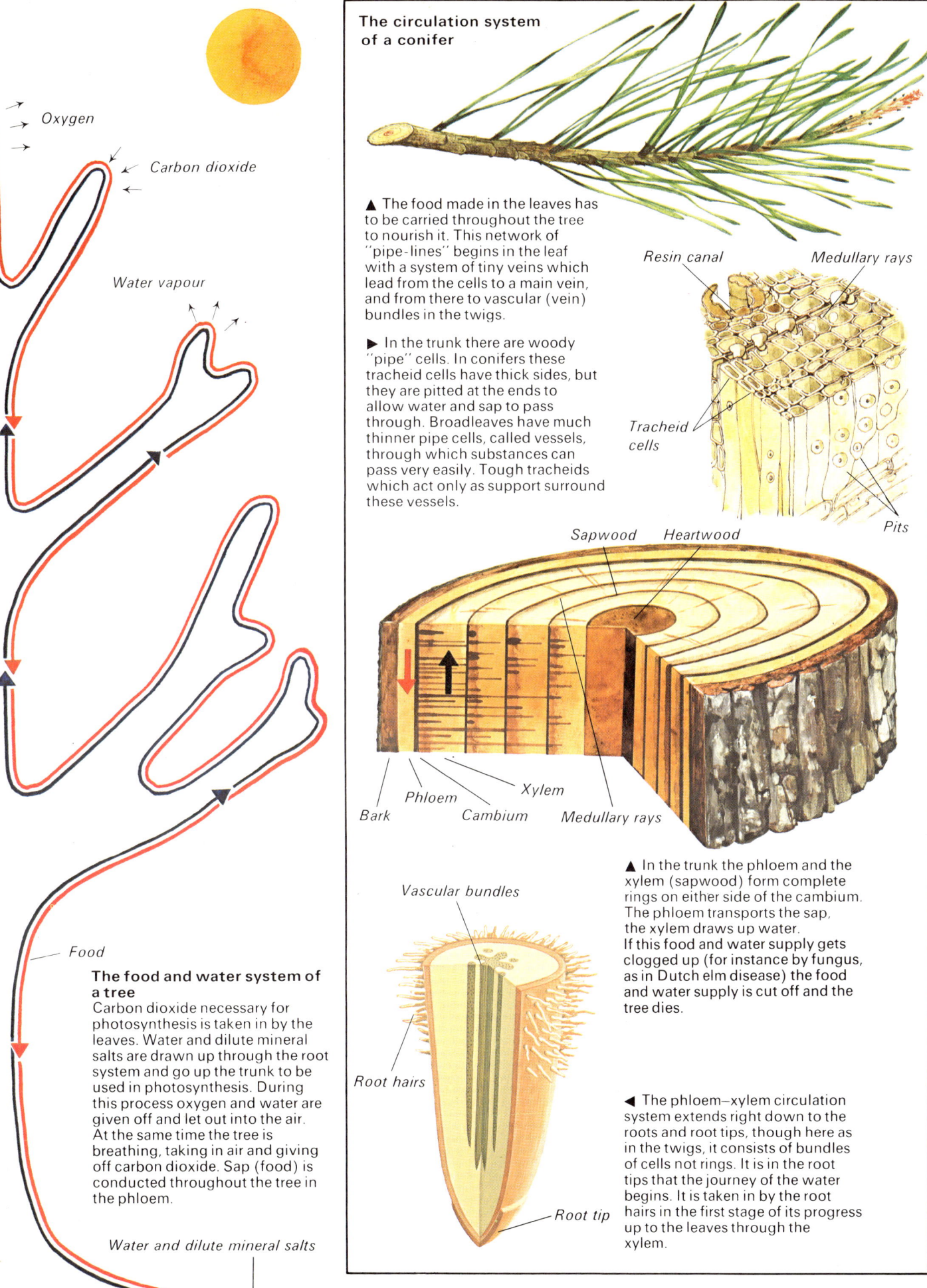

Oxygen

Carbon dioxide

Water vapour

Food

The food and water system of a tree
Carbon dioxide necessary for photosynthesis is taken in by the leaves. Water and dilute mineral salts are drawn up through the root system and go up the trunk to be used in photosynthesis. During this process oxygen and water are given off and let out into the air. At the same time the tree is breathing, taking in air and giving off carbon dioxide. Sap (food) is conducted throughout the tree in the phloem.

Water and dilute mineral salts

The circulation system of a conifer

▲ The food made in the leaves has to be carried throughout the tree to nourish it. This network of ''pipe-lines'' begins in the leaf with a system of tiny veins which lead from the cells to a main vein, and from there to vascular (vein) bundles in the twigs.

▶ In the trunk there are woody ''pipe'' cells. In conifers these tracheid cells have thick sides, but they are pitted at the ends to allow water and sap to pass through. Broadleaves have much thinner pipe cells, called vessels, through which substances can pass very easily. Tough tracheids which act only as support surround these vessels.

Resin canal

Medullary rays

Tracheid cells

Pits

Sapwood

Heartwood

Bark

Phloem

Cambium

Xylem

Medullary rays

Vascular bundles

Root hairs

Root tip

▲ In the trunk the phloem and the xylem (sapwood) form complete rings on either side of the cambium. The phloem transports the sap, the xylem draws up water.
If this food and water supply gets clogged up (for instance by fungus, as in Dutch elm disease) the food and water supply is cut off and the tree dies.

◀ The phloem–xylem circulation system extends right down to the roots and root tips, though here as in the twigs, it consists of bundles of cells not rings. It is in the root tips that the journey of the water begins. It is taken in by the root hairs in the first stage of its progress up to the leaves through the xylem.

Leaves the food makers

From seed to leaves

Seed

Cotyledons

Seed

Cotyledons

Normal leaf

Scots pine seedling

Maple seedling

Veins

In conifer species, the veins in a leaf run parallel to each other into the central midrib. In broadleaves, there is a great deal of branching and sub-branching as can be clearly seen if you look at decomposing leaves on a forest floor or at a fossil leaf like the poplar on page 5.

Conifers

Broadleaves

▲ The seeds of the **Scots pine** and **maple** are both windborne and both have wings. But however similar they look at this stage, they are soon recognizable as different kinds of tree. The cotyledons (several in the case of the pine, two for the maple) grow straight from the seed and nourish the seedling in its earliest stage, after which the tree's characteristic leaves appear.

A magnified section of a leaf

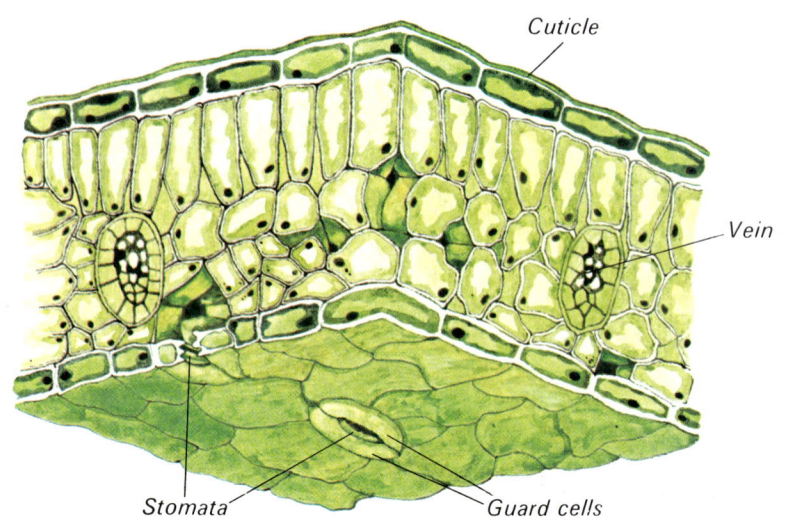

Cuticle

Vein

Stomata

Guard cells

◄ A magnified section of a leaf. The waxy outer cover, the cuticle, helps prevent the leaf from being dried out by the sun. The leaves let out excess moisture through tiny pores in their under-surface called stomata. The two guard cells which border the stomata control how much water is expelled. These cells are kidney-shaped. When there is a lot of water around, the cells are stretched tight and the hole between them is large. When there is less water around, the cells are floppier and their edges nearly touch, so that the hole is almost closed and very little water can escape.

Food is all around

Leaves, as we have seen, come in all shapes and sizes, but they all serve the same purpose: to make food. Unlike animals, plants don't have to move around to find food as their materials are all around them. Water and dissolved minerals are in the soil, carbon dioxide is in the air and sunshine is up above. If you look at a leaf under a microscope you can see lots of little holes or pores called stomata peppered over its lower surface. It is through these that the leaf takes in carbon dioxide and oxygen from the air and gives out water vapour.

The thirsty tree

A tree needs a lot of water both for food-making (photosynthesis) and to keep its "circulation" going. (A full-grown tree needs as much as 70 litres on a hot summer's day.) Water transpires or evaporates out through the stomata; on a warm day very large quantities are lost. To reduce this water loss the stomata each have two guard cells on either side of the pore which close up in the heat of the day.

The lifetime of leaves

Because trees need sunlight for photosynthesis there cannot be much activity during the winter months. The leaves of broadleaved trees with their relatively large surface area work very hard during the spring and summer months and are shed in the autumn. The evergreen pines can photosynthesize when there is less light and warmth, and the sun is lower down on the horizon. Leaves on pine trees are altogether tougher and more resistant to extremes of weather both hot and cold, but even they cannot last for ever. The average life of a conifer needle is about six years although the extraordinary triangular leaves of the monkey puzzle can stay on the tree for up to 45 years.

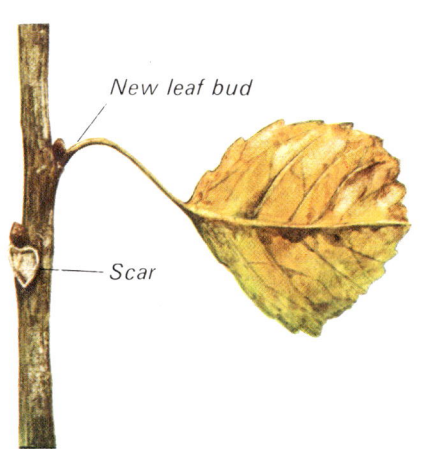

New leaf bud

Scar

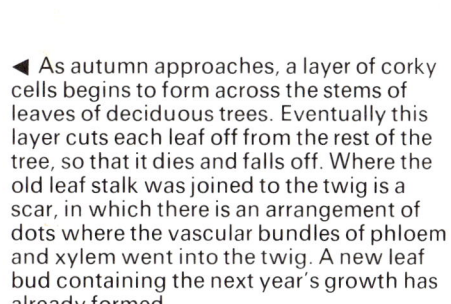

◀ As autumn approaches, a layer of corky cells begins to form across the stems of leaves of deciduous trees. Eventually this layer cuts each leaf off from the rest of the tree, so that it dies and falls off. Where the old leaf stalk was joined to the twig is a scar, in which there is an arrangement of dots where the vascular bundles of phloem and xylem went into the twig. A new leaf bud containing the next year's growth has already formed.

▲ It is in the autumn that the leaves can be said to show their true colours. The green chlorophyll decomposes and the leaves turn to their natural colours of yellow or red. They fall from the tree and drift down to the ground where their nutrients gradually leach or seep back into the soil and enrich it.

Twigs the shape of the tree

Swamp cypress

Oak

Young oak

Young swamp cypress

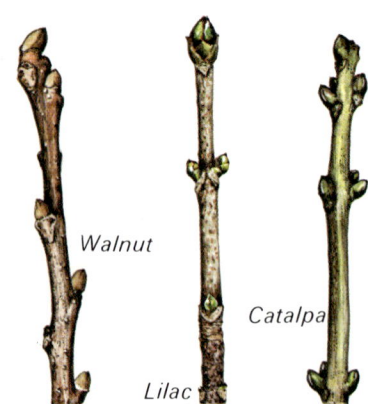

Walnut

Catalpa

Lilac

▲ Three examples of bud and leaf arrangements. Walnut leaves grow singly, one leaf and one bud climbing alternately up the twig. Lilac has its buds and leaves in pairs growing opposite one another. Catalpa has a triple formation with three buds and leaves at a time growing at intervals along the twig.

Recognizing trees in winter

The character of a tree lies in the shape of the twig, for the twig grows into a branch which sprouts more twiglets. All the twigs on the same type of tree have the same basic shape and arrangement of buds. There is the slender graceful brown twig of the beech, with its long buds, the stocky grey twig of the ash with its large, black up-tilted bud, or the crookedly angled oak twig. Experts can look at a winter twig and tell which species of tree it comes from, but for most of us the mass of twigs, branches and leaves give a general impression. From these we gradually come to recognize the characteristic tree shapes. Even if we cannot identify every twig, however, it is worth knowing about them because the twig gives the key to how a tree grows.

The resting stage

Every spring, as the weather gets sunnier and warmer the buds open up and the leaves grow. What is not so familiar is that the buds began to form the previous spring. Inside the bud, baby leaves and flowers are folded tightly together, ready to emerge the following year.

The bud is the resting stage of most trees in temperate regions. The tender new growth safely survives the hard winter protected by its bud scales. Next year's buds are almost fully formed by the summer although they will not open up until nine months later. The bud at the end of the twig is the one which extends its length and this leader grows more strongly than the other leaf and flower buds. As the twigs grow outwards, the spread of the tree gradually increases.

The branch and twig structure of deciduous trees is not concealed by the leaves.

Willow

Young willow

◀ The branch and twig structure of deciduous trees can best be seen in winter when it is not concealed by the leaves. The **common oak** twigs are all "elbows", and it has massive twisting low branches and a splendid spreading crown. The **swamp cypress** is one of the few deciduous conifers. Its central trunk persists to the top of the tree and its dense but delicate branches grow from it in an upswept manner. The **white willow** is a tall rather shapeless tree. The smaller twigs grow thickly and curve upward.

▲ This odd-looking willow with its quantities of stiff branches has been pollarded to provide a useful crop of poles and fencing. Naturally this tree would grow to 30 metres, but if the main branches are lopped off, many smaller ones take their place. Poles can be cut from it every seven years. Pollarded willows give an extra benefit in that the interlacing network of roots prevents erosion of river banks.

◀ The branches of laburnum can be trained over arches to form a beautiful tunnel of drooping yellow flower clusters in spring. Wisteria and passion flower can also be trained in this way.

▶ A hawthorn hedge is a most effective barrier and "laying" it is a skilled task — and a tough one. In winter these "living fences" are tended, the new growth partly cut through and woven in between stout stems left standing.

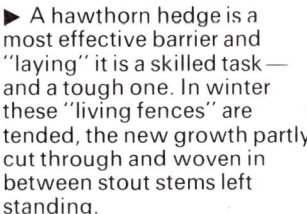

Roots the anchor

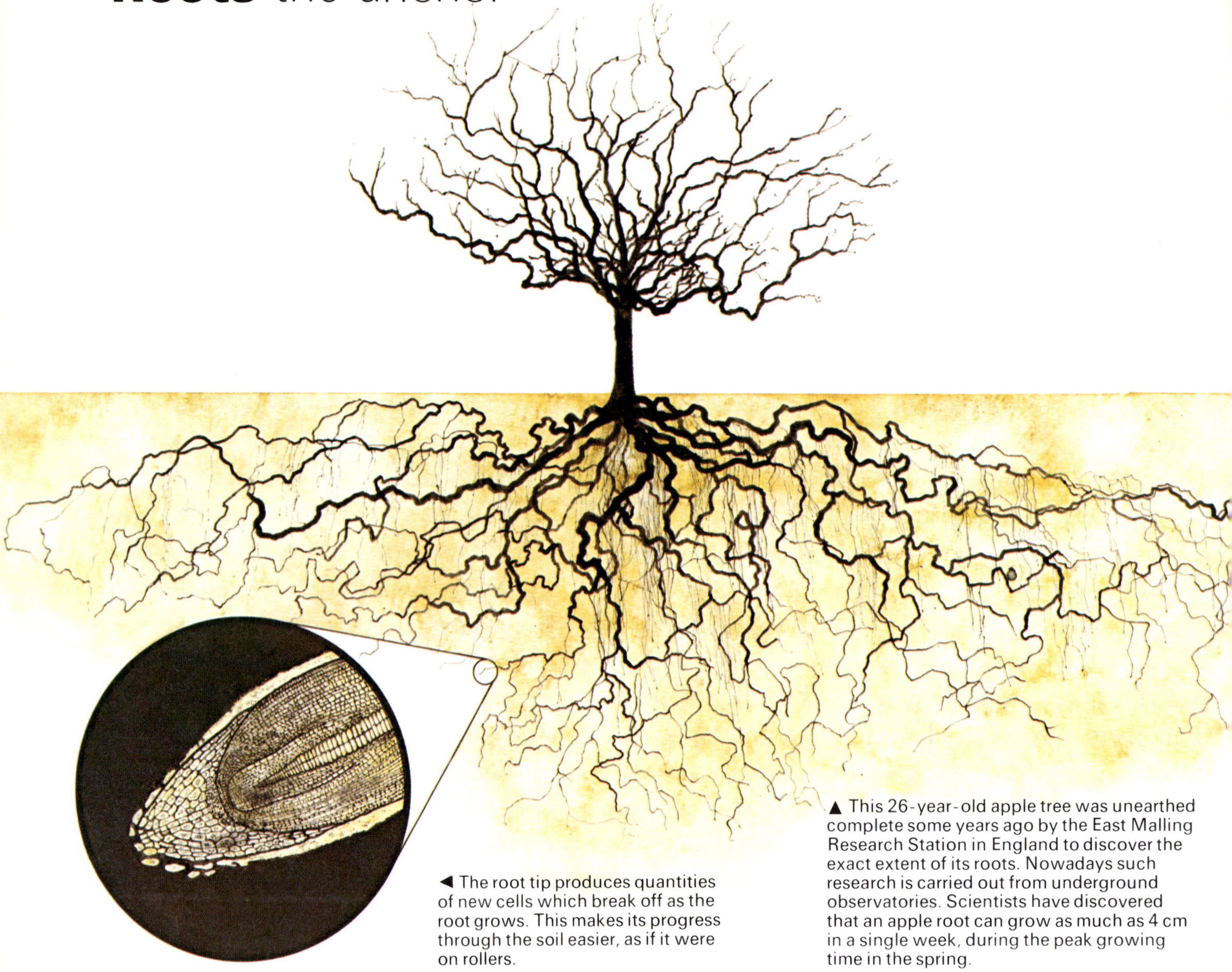

◄ The root tip produces quantities of new cells which break off as the root grows. This makes its progress through the soil easier, as if it were on rollers.

▲ This 26-year-old apple tree was unearthed complete some years ago by the East Malling Research Station in England to discover the exact extent of its roots. Nowadays such research is carried out from underground observatories. Scientists have discovered that an apple root can grow as much as 4 cm in a single week, during the peak growing time in the spring.

► Mangrove trees grow in saltwater, tidal swamps, an apparently impossible situation for any tree to flourish in. No tree can live with its roots permanently under water, cut off from an air supply. Mangroves solve this by growing "arms" through which they can breathe, up from the airless mud.

◄ Another problem is the changing tidal water level. Mangroves deal with this by growing up on "stilts". The main trunk begins high up, balanced on spidery aerial roots.

Hidden network

Something as big as a tree obviously needs a firm anchor in the soil if it is to remain upright in the face of winds and storms. So although the roots are the least obvious part of a tree, hidden as they are under the ground, they form a network as magnificent in its way as the branch structure above. In many trees the roots often extend further afield than the leaf canopy.

The tree's "water pipes"

Roots also have another vital function, the transport of water to the tree. It is the tiny ends of the root tips growing near the surface of the ground that do this through little root hairs at their tips. They push this way and that through the soil, drinking up moisture and dissolved minerals. The thick older roots no longer have hairs but serve for support anchoring the tree and as channels for water and sap from the root tips to the trunk.

It is still not fully understood exactly how the water is drawn up from the ground to the leaves high up in the tree-top. It would need a great deal of power to pump water up to such heights and the tree has no visible pump. There are several partial explanations but all we really know is that somehow it does happen.

Not all the water taken up by a tree is used for photosynthesis, some is transpired out through the stomata in the leaves. This transpiration is what makes a wood such a moist, cool place, even in the heat of a summer's day. Yet another portion of the water is used in the making of sap, which is a complex form of sugar in a watery solution.

▲ If this beech tree were not there the bank it is growing on would probably have been washed away. As it is, weather has exposed the roots.

▼ The banyan sends down aerial roots which form "trunks" to support its far-reaching branches. These trunk-roots make a one-tree forest!

The trunk telling the age

▲ Early explorers of the Amazon were amazed to see the immense size of the trees. "Very lofty and remarkable" wrote the biologist Charles Darwin "compared with those of Europe".

► A striking feature of many jungle trees is the "buttress" arrangement that spreads out from their trunks. This graceful skirt of wood is thought to be an aid to stability for very tall, shallow-rooting trees. A structure of very hard wood forms between the trunk and horizontal roots running near the surface of the ground. These buttresses may grow 2 metres or so from the base of the trunk and be equally as high.

Reading the rings

The trunk of a tree tells us not only its age and year-by-year history but also gives an idea of the annual weather conditions it had to face while it was growing. While the canopy above and the roots below are spreading, the cambium, a thin green sheath of growth cells just inside the bark, is enlarging the girth of the trunk. The cambium produces phloem cells on the outside and xylem cells on the inside. Every year a double ring of wood is made, a larger pale part for spring and a darker part representing the summer growth. In good years with plenty of sun and water, the annual rings are wide but in less favourable conditions the rings are much thinner.

It is only the outermost rings of wood near the cambium, and the phloem which are used in the transport of sap and water round the tree. This is why a hollow tree can still be vigorously alive. The darker heartwood is dead wood and serves mainly as support. The lines going crossways through the trunk are known as medullary rays and these transport food stored in special cells called parenchyma to and from the outer layers of the trunk.

Uses and abuses

People make a variety of uses, good and bad, from bark and sap. The sugary sap of the Canadian maple gives us maple syrup. Chewing gum is manufactured from the bark of sapodilla, while the "scrolls" of the warmly fragrant spice cinnamon are scraped from the bark of the cinnamon tree. The anti-malaria drug quinine comes from bark as does the deadly poison strychnine.

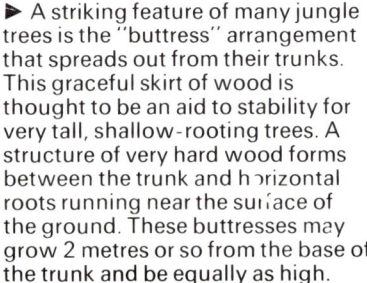

◄► The ridged outer layer of bark on trunks such as oak and elm consists of dead corky tissue. Being dead it cannot adjust to the increasing growth from inside the tree so the bark develops splits and cracks, making a characteristic pattern. The beautiful bark of the **sweet chestnut** swirls upward in a spiral of dark brown ridges. On other trees like beech, birch and cherry, the outer layer is not dead and the bark remains smooth, as on the **cherry birch**.

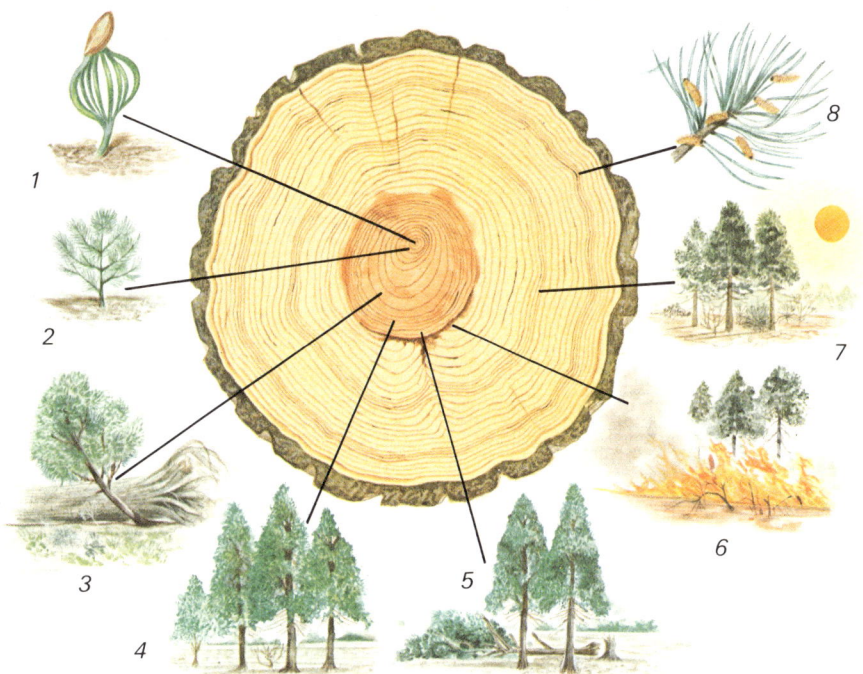

How a trunk can be a historical record

1 The beginnings of a loblolly pine. **2** Rapid early growth with broad, even rings. **3** The tree is knocked askew and grows faster on one side to get straight again. **4** Thin rings, growth is straight again but slow, due to crowding by other trees. **5** Trees around are felled and growth is good again. **6** Fire scars. **7** Narrow rings after a long, dry spell. **8** Narrow rings where insect pests slow growth.

▲ One of the most exciting archaeological finds of recent years has been a number of writings on birch bark. In medieval Russia birch bark was the least costly of writing materials and it was used even after paper was available. Writing was scratched on to the bark with a sharp instrument.

▲ The evergreen cork oak is our main source of cork. Fortunately it is one of the few trees which does not die when debarked and the thick cork bark can be stripped every 10-15 years.

◄ Flowers and fruit of cocoa grow directly from the main trunk and larger branches of the tree. Between 25 to 50 cocoa beans are embedded in the pulp of the fruit.

► Most conifers produce resins which protect the trees when the bark is wounded. People too have an interest in resin because it contains two useful substances, turpentine and rosin. The greatest amount of resin can be "tapped" from pines that grow in hot, dry regions. The bark is cut and the resin which flows out is collected and processed to separate the turpentine and rosin.

Paper from wood

Paper to suit all purposes

Paper is perhaps the world's most important wood product. It is difficult to imagine our civilization without books, newspapers, toilet rolls and all the other paper products. About half the world's timber harvest goes into paper making.

Papers for different purposes are of varying qualities, and need to be treated in different ways. Additives are put into the wood pulp in varying amounts according to the type of paper required.

▲ Thousands of logs, gathered into a solid mass by an enclosing boom, are towed away to the pulp mill where they will be debarked and reduced to a pulp. The pulp is then dried out and ready for use in the paper-making process.

▶ China clay gives strength to paper, while size makes the paper waterproof, so it does not act like blotting paper when ink is put on. For a fine smooth finish as in writing paper the roll of dried paper is calendered, or passed through abrasive rollers which take away any roughnesses on the paper's surface.

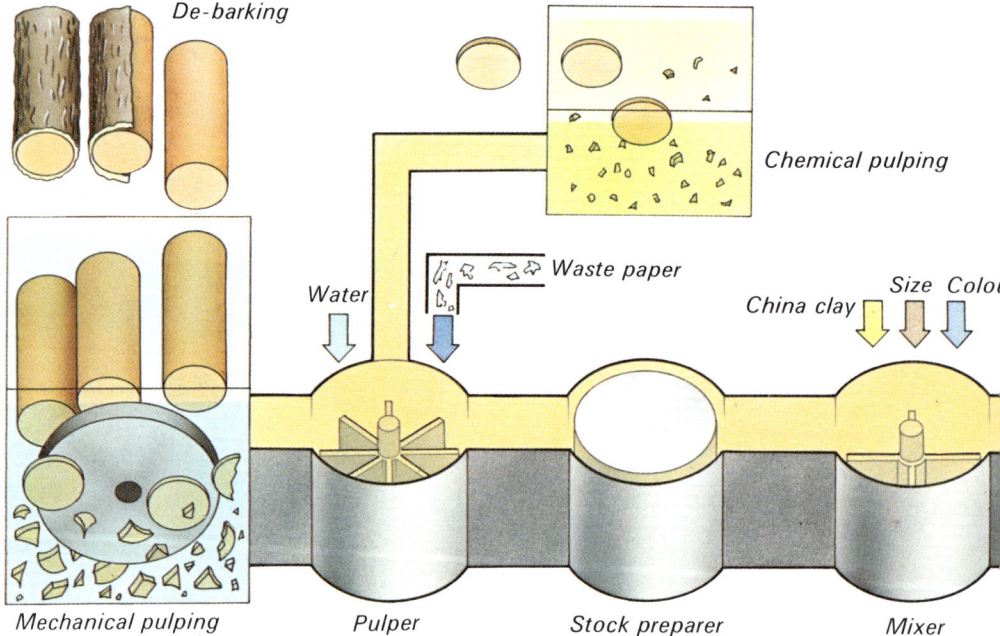

De-barking

Chemical pulping

Water

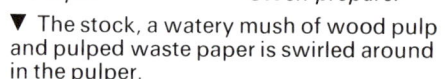
Waste paper

China clay   Size   Colo[u]r

Mechanical pulping   Pulper   Stock preparer   Mixer

▼ Logs have to have their bark removed, after which the wood is chipped and fed into a chemical digester before pulping.

▼ The stock, a watery mush of wood pulp and pulped waste paper is swirled around in the pulper.

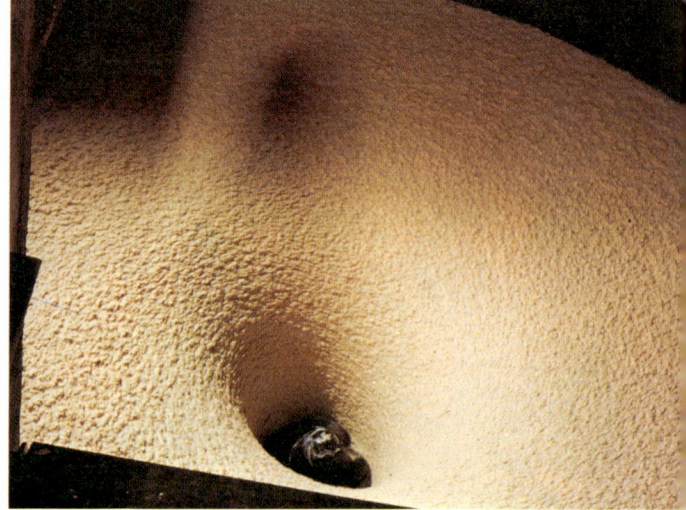

Making rayon

◀ The man-made material rayon was originally known as "tree silk" when it was developed in the 1890s. Wood pulp is broken down by chemical treatment into viscose, a substance which looks like treacle.

▼ The viscose is then drawn through tiny holes in a "spinnerette" and solidified into rayon threads by hardening chemicals. The thread can then be spun into material in the same way as a natural fibre such as linen or wool.

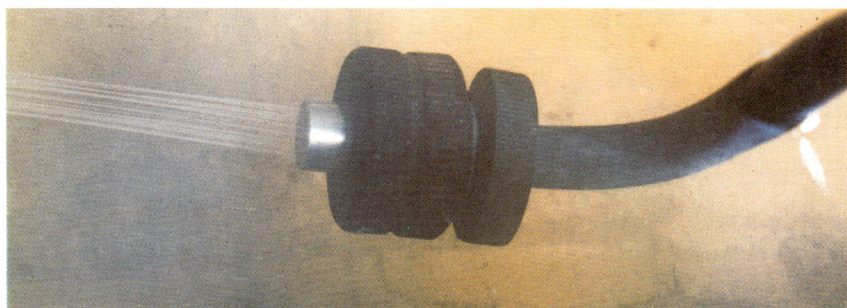

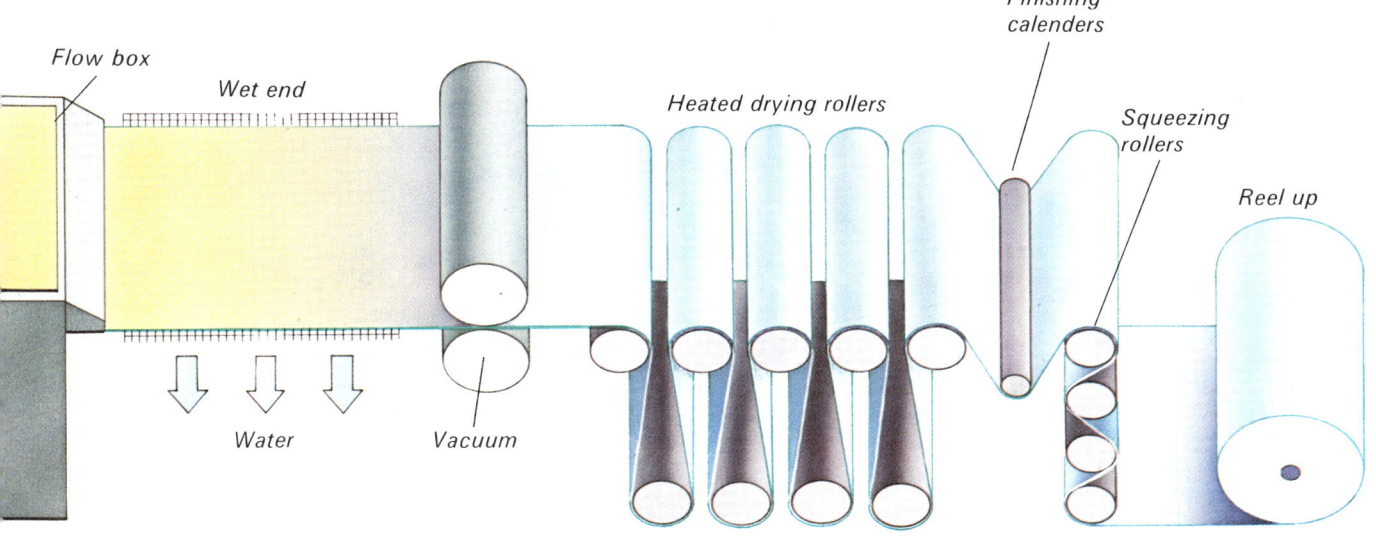

Flow box
Wet end
Heated drying rollers
Finishing calenders
Squeezing rollers
Reel up
Water
Vacuum

▼ The wet end, a moving belt of wire mesh on which stock is spread. The water drains through, leaving a loose fibrous web.

▼ Huge rollers squeeze out more water from the web and press the fibres closer together. Heated rollers finish the drying.

Flowers the essential aid to pollination

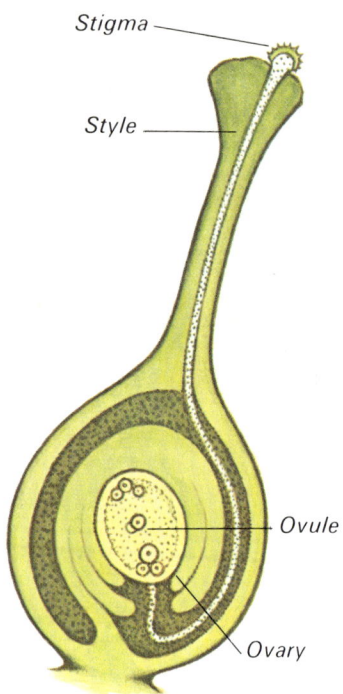

Stigma

Style

Ovule

Ovary

▲ For pollination to take place, a grain of pollen has to land on the stigma of a flower. If the pollen and stigma are from the same kind of plant, the pollen grain will then grow a tube which goes right down the style until it reaches the ovary. The "male" part inside the pollen grain will then join with the "female" part inside the ovule to form a seed. This is called fertilization.

Lime

Scots pine

◄ Pollen grains are protected by a tough, waxy outer layer. The surface of the lime pollen grain is regular but rough so it will stick to pollinating insects. Pollen grains of the Scots pine have balloon-like "wings" which help it to float on the air in its journey to the female cone.

The beginnings of the seed

For people, the appearance of catkins and pussy willow is a welcome sign of spring. To the trees, these and other more showy flowers like the horse chestnut and magnolia have a greater significance. They represent the first stage in the seed-producing cycle. Flowers contain the sexual organs of a tree. Their male and female parts are sometimes carried on separate flowers, sometimes contained in the same flower.

Pollination takes place when the pollen released from the male part comes to rest on the stigma of the female part. The potential seeds, the ovules, are then fertilized and the baby seed begins to grow.

A chance in a million!

There are various ways by which the pollen reaches the female flower: wind, insects, birds, even bats play their part. Wind-pollinated trees, which include the majority of the trees in the temperate forests, release vast quantities of pollen into the air, some of which will float down onto the female stigma. This may seem rather a hit-and-miss system, but early in the year there is always a wind, and the passage of the pollen grains is not obstructed by leaves. Besides, the pollen cloud is of such high density that there is a good chance that at least a few grains will find their goal. It has been estimated that one birch catkin produces about $5\frac{1}{2}$ million pollen grains!

Wind-pollinated trees generally have inconspicuous flowers, but trees depending on insects to carry pollen from one tree to another have seductive petals or scents to guide the insects to them. In tropical forests, where the air is completely still, you find trees of indescribable colour and variety. They attract huge populations of insects and small birds such as hummingbirds and sunbirds, who feed off the nectar in the flowers one after the other, pollinating them as they go.

▲ There are many insect pollinators, of which the best known is the bee. In the windless tropical forests, flowers are pollinated by a huge variety of insects including ants and butterflies, but there are more unusual pollinators such as hummingbirds and bats. This Gambian fruit bat is visiting a tropical tree.

▼ The mass of tiny flowers on this birch catkin release millions of pollen grains into the breeze. Male catkins form in the autumn and mature in spring. The female catkins are carried on the same tree and are shorter and stiffer.

▲ In early summer the rhododendron is covered with bright flowers which attract insects to them to ensure pollination. In the temperate climates of Europe and North America, the rhododendron flourishes as a large shrub, but in the Himalayas it grows on a single trunk as a clearly defined tree, growing as high as 30 metres.

▲ The magnolia has a long history. It was one of the first flowering trees to develop. Magnolias have what are known as "perfect" flowers. This means that there are male and female parts in the same flower. The parts mature at different times to avoid self-pollination, which is less desirable than a cross between different trees. The lovely waxy blooms attract insect pollinators.

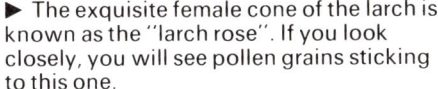

► The exquisite female cone of the larch is known as the "larch rose". If you look closely, you will see pollen grains sticking to this one.

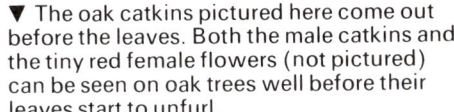

▼ Male and female cones of spruce become mature at different times to avoid self-pollination. The larger female cone begins erect and droops as it ripens. Male cones produce such heavy quantities of pollen that showers of the yellow dust fall from the tree in spring.

▼ The oak catkins pictured here come out before the leaves. Both the male catkins and the tiny red female flowers (not pictured) can be seen on oak trees well before their leaves start to unfurl.

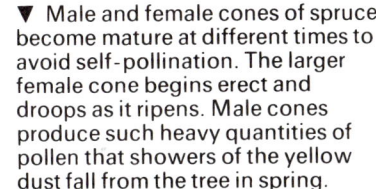

Fruits and seeds the start of a new tree

The variety of fruits

Coconut

Orange

Peach

Beechnut

Lime

▲ Seeds and fruits come in a variety of shapes and sizes, each kind adapted for dispersal in its own environment. The coconut fruit has a fibrous husk which enables it to float from island to island. (What we buy in the shops is just the seed of the coconut.) Lime seeds are carried by wind. Beechnuts are dropped or buried by birds and mammals, as are the seeds of orange and peach when the flesh has been eaten.

One of the oldest foods

Fruit growing is nothing new. The earliest civilizations grew trees for fruits, nuts and oil. Nearly 6,000 years ago the Pharoahs were planting trees and employing "foresters" to tend them.

Many fruits which originated in the East have over the centuries been introduced to other regions. One of the most familiar fruits, the apple, originated in Afghanistan. Citrus fruits from Persia, oranges, lemons and limes, were introduced to the Mediterranean and are now valuable crops not only there, but in North America, Australia and southern Africa. Such fruits are important because they may be stored for a long time without deteriorating. Others, like mangos and avocados, are vital to the areas in which they are grown but don't keep and are expensive to export.

How seeds are dispersed

▲ The succulent flesh of these rowan berries will be digested but the seed will be passed out intact in the blackbird's droppings.

▲ Some seeds like the poplar have a fluffy attachment which carries them away on the wind.

Seeds and new trees

Trees produce huge quantities of fruit and seeds. Only a few of these seeds ever grow into new trees because young seedlings are very vulnerable and are often trampled or eaten by animals. An oak tree may produce as many as 50,000 acorns but perhaps only one of these will grow into a new tree. The rest feed animals and birds. A single woodpigeon can eat about 140 acorns in a single day.

Seeds have to get away from the the parent tree in order to grow. Some seeds are fluffy or winged and can be carried away by the wind, others like the alder are swept away by water. Yet other seeds are cased in succulent fleshy fruit which attracts animals and birds to eat them; the seed is then excreted some distance away, perhaps in a place where it can grow up.

▲ Alders like damp places and are usually found by rivers. Alder seeds are buoyant and float away on the water.

▲ Witch hazel seeds are enclosed in a container which explodes, catapulting the ripe seeds out.

► The woodcuts of trees were a striking feature of this German herbal, the *Kreuter Buch*, published in 1546. Herbals of this era had recognizable and life-like representations of plants, which showed a concern for botanical accuracy.

▼ This tradition continued, as is seen by these illustrations of pomegranate, fig, apricot and cherry from a French book on trees which appeared in the early 1800s. Many fine artists were employed for such botanical works. They produced illustrations of considerable beauty which were also precise in their detail.

Vierdt Theyl
Nußbaum. Cap. xxxiij.

Nußbaum heysset auff Latinische spraach Iuglans, auff Griechisch Caryon basilicon, das ist / Nux regia. Er wirt auch genent Nux persica, von den Persis, von welchen er erstlich ist her komen. Den Griechischen namen Caryon, hat er bekommen / dieweil er hauptflüß machet / den jenigen so under jhm schlaffen / umb des starcken geruchs willen seiner bletter. Seine frucht nennt man auch Nuß und Welschnuß / und ist der frucht dreierlei geschlechte. Die ersten seind die grossen Pferdsnuß oder Roßnuß / welche einer faust groß werden / und heyssen bein Latinischen Nuces equinæ. Die andern seind die mittelmessigen/

Apricot

Pomegranate

Cherry

Fig

Breeding the best

▲ To make sure of strong growth and good yield in fruit trees, shoots (scions) of best quality fruit stocks are grafted onto a related variety with strong roots. This mature tree still bears the sign of its "trunk transplant" in the form of a bulge where the join was made.

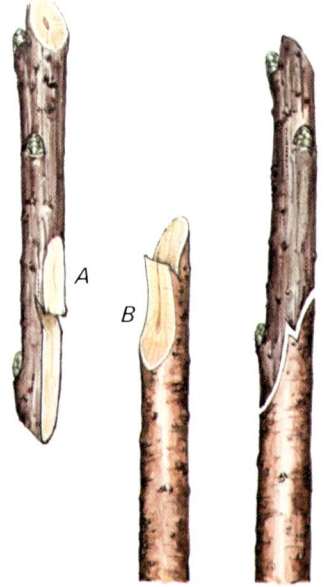

▲ There are a number of different ways of grafting but the principle is to connect two living parts of plants so that they form a growing union. In the diagram above, the scion A is matched to a branch or trunk B. The two parts are then bound together and left to unite and grow.

Aiming for quantity and quality

Economic success with trees depends on breeding the best for your purpose whether for fruit, timber, or a sap or bark product. The general aim is to produce the most vigorous type of tree with high productivity, which is also resistant to disease and pests.

The tendency in fruit-growing today is to breed smaller trees and to plant them much closer together. (The apple trees of the future may look like tomato plants rather than orchard trees.) This is to save the labour costs of harvesting and maintenance, the most expensive item on a fruit farmer's budget. To make sure that the whole crop is of a uniform standard, nearly all fruit and nut trees are grown from grafts or cuttings from trees that have been specially selected.

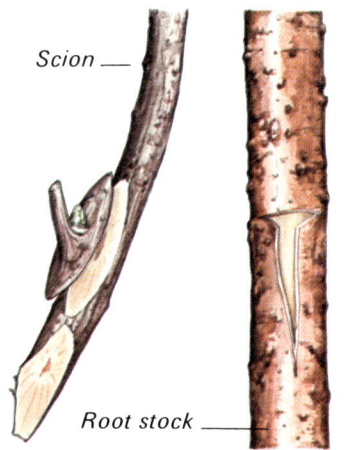

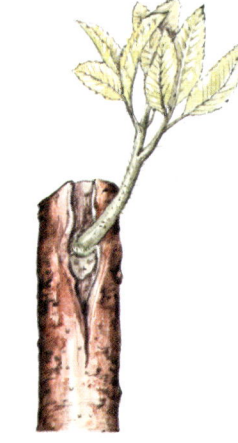

Scion —

Root stock —

▲ Bud grafting. A slice of wood with a bud is removed from the scion and inserted into a slit in the bark of the root stock. This is bound up and left to "take". When it has begun to grow, the upper growth of the root stock is cut off to encourage the bud to develop into a strong shoot. A shoot like this can grow over a metre in its first year!

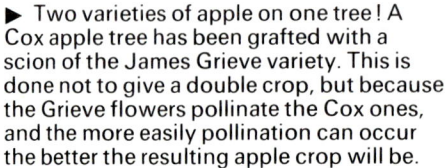

▶ Two varieties of apple on one tree! A Cox apple tree has been grafted with a scion of the James Grieve variety. This is done not to give a double crop, but because the Grieve flowers pollinate the Cox ones, and the more easily pollination can occur the better the resulting apple crop will be.

Fewer varieties for sale

It is arguable that the taste suffers when there is such an emphasis on productivity. Certainly although there is a greater variety of fruits on record, there are actually fewer varieties grown in quantity and less choice for the buyer.

Breeding for timber

Conifer planting is usually done from seed. This seed is very carefully controlled. Two vigorous parent trees are selected and cross bred. The hardy hybrid larch has the fine wood of the European larch yet grows quickly like its Japanese parent. Latest methods of cross-pollination and grafting mean that parent trees can be growing long distances from each other. When a desirable strain has been established, a "seed bank" is set up for future use.

▲ These larch "roses", the female cones of specially chosen trees, are ready for pollination. They are protected by covers so that no pollen other than that selected by the forester can find its way in to fertilize the cones.

▲ Male cones from selected trees have been gathered and the pollen extracted from them is injected into the container surrounding the female cone. By this means an exact cross breed is assured and the seeds which follow will go into a "seed bank".

► Collecting seeds. Gathering ripe cones from a Japanese larch.

▼ Pine needles present a feast for the pine looper, a moth whose caterpillars occasionally reach plague proportions and strip entire trees of their leaves.

▼ Aerial spraying with insecticides like DDT is sometimes used to kill pine loopers and other pests. This method is now thought to do more harm than good however, as it poisons *all* insects not just pests. Wildlife which eats insects is also affected. And when done on a large scale spraying results in widespread pollution of rivers and a chain of death for wildlife.

The natural forests of the world

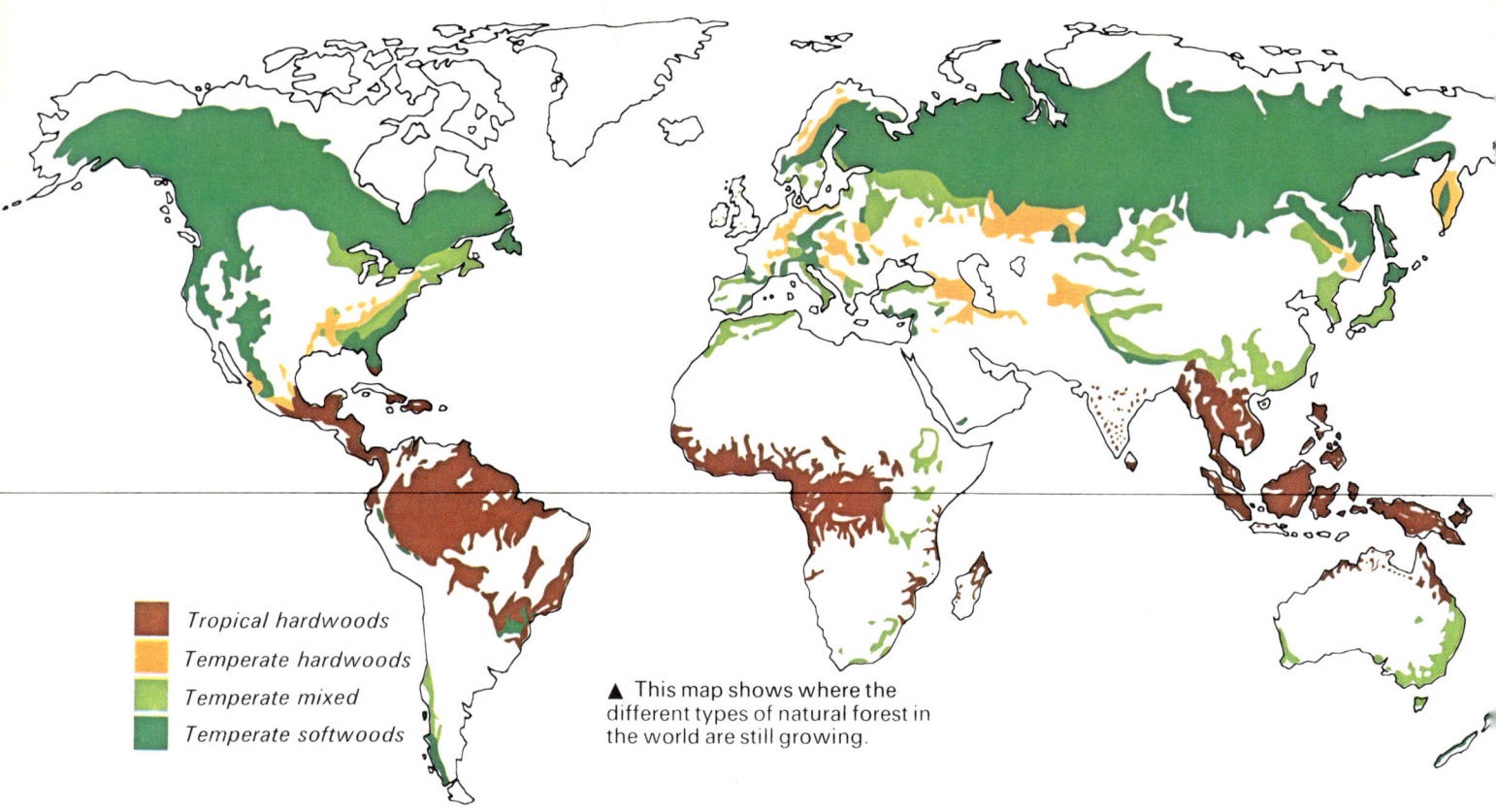

Tropical hardwoods
Temperate hardwoods
Temperate mixed
Temperate softwoods

▲ This map shows where the different types of natural forest in the world are still growing.

The destruction of natural habitats

Vast areas of Europe and North America were once completely covered by trees, yet today only a few natural conifer forests remain untouched by people. It is necessary now to seek natural forests in the least inviting and accessible parts of the world. Now even trackless forests in Africa and South America are daily being pillaged for luxury timbers. In Costa Rica a hectare of land is cleared of trees every two hours.

People's greed and thoughtlessness is destroying irreplaceable forests which have grown there for thousands of years. The plant life which takes over the clearings is of a different kind altogether. It would take thousands more years to re-establish the old forests even if this were still possible. Ancient woods have evolved a delicate balance of life, and deprived of this habitat, plants and animals soon become extinct. It would be particularly sad if this were to happen in the tropical forests both because of their great variety of plants and animals and their unique history. It is generally thought that flowering plants and trees originated in tropical forests and migrated north and south-ward.

The unique life of tropical forests

There is still an amazing profusion of life in tropical forests. New plant and animal species are continually being discovered (often just before they are wiped out). Whereas temperate forests are usually dominated by a single type of tree with no more than ten species throughout, in a tropical forest it is not unusual to find 100 species in a hectare!

One would think that by now the world would have realized the dangers of destroying the balance of nature in these unique natural forests. But it is by no means sure that the conservationists will win their battle against the forces of commerce.

▶ **The world's most varied habitat.**

The Malayan tropical forest harbours an incredible variety of plant and animal life, perhaps the most abundant in the world. From beneath the forest floor where the bamboo rat has its burrow to the very top of the tree canopy where exotic butterflies flit, each level has its own typical residents, of which a tiny selection is shown opposite. Although insects and animals are mobile, they, like plants, tend to inhabit a particular zone which suits their needs.

▶ **Animals of the Malayan forests**

Crested swifts spend most of their time in the air above the canopy, catching insects on the wing.
Colugo The colugo's folds of skin enable it to glide from tree to tree, feeding on vegetation.
Hornbill This bird's strong bill pushes up through tangled foliage to reach fruit on thin twigs.
Lar gibbon This agile gibbon lives mainly in the middle layer but goes up to the canopy to feed on fruit.
Banded linsang A hunter with sheathed claws like a cat, the linsang springs out on rats and mice.
Pigtail macaque Bands of 30 to 50 of these aggressive monkeys live in low branches and on the ground.
Tree mouse One of eight species of Asiatic mice which live in trees.
Clouded leopard This rarely-seen night-hunter preys mainly on birds, rodents and small monkeys.
Reticulated python The world's largest snake, this python feeds mainly on birds and small mammals.
Bamboo rats live in underground burrows, feeding on bamboo roots.
Malayan bear and **Malayan porcupine** Two of the numerous larger plant-eating mammals inhabiting the Malayan jungle. Others include elephants, rhinos, deer and pigs. There are fewer species of large carnivores such as tigers and leopards.

Animals of the Malayan forests

Crested swifts

Colugo

Great India hornbill

Lar gibbon

Banded linsang

Pigtail macaque

Tree mouse

Clouded leopard

Reticulated python

Bamboo rat

Malayan bear

Malayan porcupine

Plant layers in tropical forests

The very highest trees of the tropical forest are widely spaced (**A**). The next layer is still quite sunny (**B**). But beneath this is the densest tree cover (**C**) through which almost no light can penetrate to the trees and plants lower down (**D**). Plants growing beneath this dense layer have to adapt to shade or find a means of reaching light. The lianas twine their way to sunlight up trunks and branches. Another way of making sure of survival is to tap someone else's food supply, which is what the spectacular raff-lesia does; it feeds on the roots of lianas. The strangler fig eventually kills the tree around which it grows. It starts life as a seed dropped in the upper branches like many of the aerial orchids, but its roots grow down to the ground and eventually enclose the host tree completely, causing its death.

A

B

C

D

Cauliflorous flower

Liana

Strangler fig

Rafflesia

29

The woods we plant

▲ Land used for the plantation of conifers is often on hillsides not suitable as farmland. Conifers prefer a less rich soil, but this entails some precarious ploughing.

▶ In this method of transplanting, seedlings are inserted by hand. The preparation of the soil, the digging of trenches and the earthing over of the roots are done mechanically by tractor-drawn implements. The seedlings have been raised in extensive seedbeds.

▼ Fire is one of the greatest dangers to forestry plantations. This fire in Germany in 1975 raged for several weeks and destroyed millions of trees before it was brought under control.

Trees for the future

Wood is of enormous economic importance. The annual income of the world's timber crop is almost double that of steel. Wood too has one important advantage over mineral resources: it is renewable. Just as long as people remember that they have to plant as well as fell trees, it is possible to have the benefits of wood for ever.

Very few people though see forests simply in terms of their economic value as timber. Forests have been cared for and enjoyed by people for centuries. Some of the richest and most varied woodland habitats date back several centuries when wealthy landowners planted large numbers of different trees, often importing new varieties from other countries to do so.

A home for wildlife

Woods, whether planted or natural, provide a home for many animals and plants. Different kinds of forest have a different flora and fauna. Broadleaved forests have more species because they allow more light to penetrate than the conifers and so more plants can grow on the forest floor. These plants in turn support a greater variety of animals. In the past conifer plantations have been criticized as mere financial ventures that disregarded both wildlife and people. Conifers were planted in close uniform rows that made the forests dark and gloomy. Nowadays conifer plantations are more openly spaced with broadleaves often planted at their edges. Another encouraging fact is that the latest surveys show that as conifer forests grow to maturity, they shelter more wildlife than was originally supposed.

Deciduous forest in spring

All kinds of birds inhabit deciduous woodland over a year. The jay is thought to be partly responsible for the spread of oakwood: it often buries the acorns it feeds on. Woodpeckers and tree-creepers feed off insects in trees and branches. Seven species of the migrant warblers can also be heard in these woods in summer.

Many plants grow in the comparative light of deciduous woods, particularly in spring, before the leaves shade the ground. Primroses, bluebells and wood anemones are just a few. Shrubs like hazel and elder also flourish. The wood is a home too for mammals such as woodmice, squirrels and shrews.

Jay

Greater spotted woodpecker

Oak

Ivy, lichens and ferns grow on the trunks and lower branches of trees. Many hundreds of insects make their home in woods; caterpillars, beetles, bugs, wasps and flies are just a few. They can cause serious damage to the trees, but also provide food for animals and birds.

Grey squirrel

Woodmouse

Pine marten

Crossbills

Treecreeper

Long-eared owl

Roe deer

Coniferous forest in autumn

Coniferous woods are darker and denser than deciduous woods. Many animal species are common to both sorts of wood like the tree creeper on the bark. Some actually prefer conifer woods like the tiny goldcrest or the crossbill, a finch whose specialized bill makes short work of ripe cones. Deer take refuge in the quiet of these woods and on occasion a rare creature like a pine-marten may be seen.

The ground is almost bare of green plants due to lack of light and an infertile carpet of needles. Coniferous woodland does, however, support a rich variety of fungi, such as the brightly coloured fly agaric and the large, flat-tabled fungi. There are also a great many insect pests such as the pine hawkmoth and the longhorn beetle, whose larvae may attack living trees.

Bracket fungus

Goldcrest

Fly agaric

31

The solitary tree plays its part

Room for expansion

In forests trees concentrate their growth upwards to reach the sunlight, but when they grow in open spaces such as fields or hedgerows, the lower branches too develop, growing outward to catch the sun. A tree on its own can fill out to its own individual shape. Even the thin spire of a conifer such as larch can take on a billowy form as a solitary tree.

Fashion and trees

Growing new kinds of tree has given pleasure to people throughout history. As early as 1200 BC, Rameses, one of many garden-loving Pharoahs, was planting trees and shrubs so people "should sit under their shade". As with everything else, there were fashions in trees. In 17th-century Europe topiary trees were the rage, with trees such as box and yew cut into "shapes of beasts" or "pyramidy or sugar loaf or like a mushroom top". As people travelled and discovered new lands they brought back with them new plants, and many trees took remarkably well to being transplanted in places very different from their native soil.

Planting for a purpose

Fashion was of little importance to farmers whose concern was for sturdy hedges and trees for timber. Hawthorn trees kept clipped made good hedging while a few trees like oak and elm were allowed to grow to maturity for timber.

▶ Given a bit of space even naturally spare trees like the Scots pine will assume a fuller, more rounded shape. Any species of tree growing on its own is more likely to grow into a fine specimen than one surrounded by others. In the past particularly fine old trees, conspicuous for their size, were used as boundary markers or local landmarks.

▼ Trees on motorway embankments not only make driving less bleak but keep the bank sides firm. Several factors must be taken into account in choosing the types of tree to plant. Some are more resistant than others to pollution from car exhaust fumes. The trees must also look right in the general landscape. This group of schoolchildren is planting conifers in Wales.

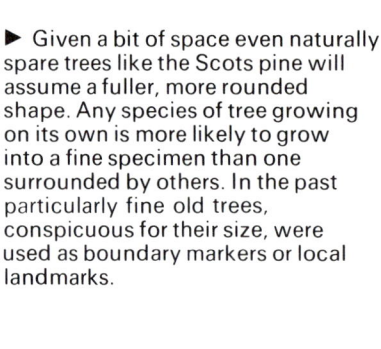

▲ The extraordinary looking monkey puzzle was not known outside its native Chile until 1795. The trees took surprisingly well to European soil and became all the fashion for gardens in the 19th century.

▶ A "heavenly" view for the occupants of these long lines of flats? The saplings are young trees of heaven which grow into lovely billowing trees with long fronds of leaves up to about a metre in length.

◀ Tree saviours. Five trees were due to be cut down in the process of building a new underground station in Amsterdam. People of the neighbourhood defended their trees by perching in the branches and refusing to come down.

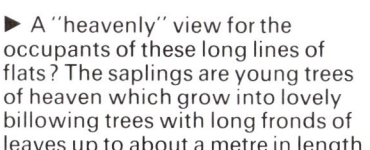

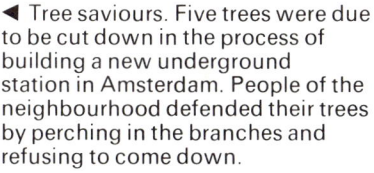

▲ Transplanting mature trees takes considerable skill. A sizeable portion of the roots and soil is 'bandaged' firmly in a frame, which is then cut away. The tree (in this case 30 tonnes of ginkgo) is transported to its new home where an ample hole has been dug, and lowered gently into position. The tree will then need careful feeding and tending until its roots settle in and grow again.

Myths and legends built around trees

Larger than life

Trees are the largest living things in the world but this fact alone does not account for their importance in myth and religion. They have an indefinable influence which has always caught people's imagination.

Religious symbols

Scandinavians worshipped the sacred ash whose branches reached to heaven and whose roots went down to hell. The Druids specially esteemed the oak and yew, the Egyptians, a fig-tree. A "Tree of Life" has a place in many religions. One legend says that when Adam and Eve were expelled from the Garden of Eden, Adam took a cutting from the Tree of Life and grew it. Christ's cross was supposed to have been made from the wood of the tree which Adam grew. The custom of Christmas trees may be derived from ancient tree worship.

The tree of Judas

There are legends too about the tree upon which Judas hanged himself. In Sicily it is thought to have been the tamarisk tree, which since the deed has grown only as a stunted shrub. The Russian story is that it was the aspen, which has trembled ever since. Other stories accord the doubtful honour to the elder and the fig.

Trees in history

Plants as grand and long-lived as trees are a natural focus for history and legend. There are stories about trees commemorating all kinds of historical events. It was believed that the ancient ruling family of Manchu would thrive in China as long as an arborvitae tree flourished in the imperial garden at Pekin. Alexander the Great *and* his whole army was said to have sheltered under the sacred banyan tree in India.

▲ The Greek god Apollo was smitten with love for the beautiful nymph Daphne who, however, did not care for him at all. The more Apollo pursued her the more violently she fled. When Apollo at last caught up with her she cried for help and was changed into a laurel tree. Apollo embraced the tree and declared that it would always be fresh and green as his love for Daphne which would never fade. From then on the laurel has been an evergreen.

◄ Not so different from modern forestry methods? In the ancient temple of Assur-bani-pal, a god hand pollinates a mythical tree of life. In one hand he carries a bag of pollen, in the other a kind of powder puff.

► Did truth seem as strange as legend in the time of the early herbals ? The monkey eating peaches probably seemed as odd as the barnacle-goose tree. In fact 15th- and 16th-century botanists took great pains to be well informed. Francis Drake collected foreign plants for the herbalist l'Ecluse, who himself is said to have set a Turkish captive free to gather new plants for him.

▼ This legendary barnacle-goose tree from a Gerard's Herbal of 1597 was an amazing confusion of ideas. It was believed that the tree sprouted barnacle shells from which geese hatched out. The legend grew out of observation of barnacles on driftwood. Barnacles in fact have a feathery appendage and this was mistakenly thought to be the first feather of the baby bird.

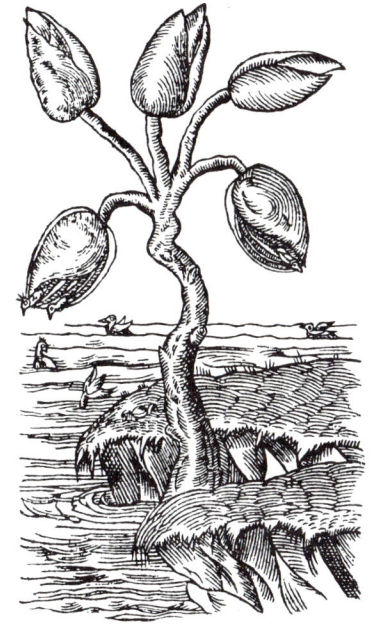

▲ The coming of spring used to be a real cause for celebration after the hardship of winter. In this 19th-century print an elaborate maypole is the centre of the gaiety enjoyed by both rich and poor.

◄ The legendary "poison tree", the Bohun Upas, was much feared. It was believed this tree killed medieval travellers by giving out noxious fumes. Hostile tribes used to tie prisoners to its trunk as a means of execution. Any living thing within range of the tree would fall asleep, never to wake.

The forest community

A vast number of creatures can live alongside one another in a forest, feeding off different plants and at different levels. Each has its own place so they don't compete too much for the available food and shelter. This table shows how the community works.

Trees and shrubs

Leaves
eaten by — larvae of moths (e.g. green tortrix on oak; oak eggar on bramble, hazel and ivy but *not* on oak) larvae of sawflies
sap sucked by — aphids (e.g. oak leaf aphid)
mined by — larvae of moths and other insects

Bark
eaten by — rabbits
common voles
bored by — larvae of weevils (e.g. oak bark beetle)

Fruits and seeds
eaten by — birds (e.g. robin, green woodpecker) mammals (mice, squirrels, voles)
bored by — larvae of weevils
sucked by — shieldbugs

Galls
caused by — over 50 different insects including various gall wasps causing oak apples, oak marble galls and spangle galls

Field and ground layers

Leaves and stems
eaten by — rabbits
slugs
snails
larvae of insects
sap sucked by — aphids
capsid bugs
mined by — larvae of insects

Roots
eaten by — larvae of insects
roundworms

Fruits and seeds
eaten by — mice
birds (hedge sparrow, yellowhammer)
squirrels
sucked by — insects (capsid bugs on ferns)

Pollen and/or nectar
taken by — butterflies
bees

Leaf litter
is fed on by — many species including:
snails
millipedes
springtails
woodlice

Fungi
are fed on by — adults and larvae of many insects (e.g. fungus beetle, boletus beetle)

The animals above are all herbivores, feeding directly on plants. These herbivores themselves provide food for the carnivorous and insectivorous woodland animals. Insects provide food for birds like thrushes and woodpeckers, mammals such as hedgehogs and shrews, spiders and insectivorous insects such as ladybirds. These in turn may fall victim (along with the herbivores) to the birds and beasts of prey—owls, hawks, stoats and foxes. Nothing is wasted in this community; even excrement produces food for dung beetles and dung flies, and dead animals attract carrion feeders like sexton beetles and blowfly larvae.

The spangle gall of the Cynips wasp

The caterpillar of the buff tip moth

These galleries are made by elm-bark beetles which carry Dutch elm disease.

Fly agaric is found in many kinds of wood

The oak-apple gall of Biorhiza wasp. The pins show some of the holes where the young wasps crawled out.

Leaf miner insects feed *inside* leaves

Beech tuft fungus lives off lower branches

This bracket fungus feeds off living trees

Oak

Beech

Elm

Woodland is a marvellously rich habitat. From tree top to leaf litter and root level plants and creatures live and die. But their lives are not separate; this mass of life has an internal balance. If too many insects ate their leaves the trees would die—but birds eat insects. Fungi and bacteria feed off dead plants and animals, decomposing them and returning them to the soil—insects feed off the fungi. All these living things are linked together in a complex web of life.

This centipede lives in beech leaf litter

Tree sculpture

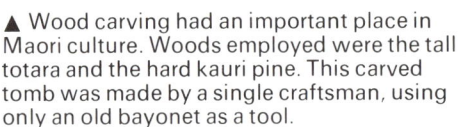
▲ Wood carving had an important place in Maori culture. Woods employed were the tall totara and the hard kauri pine. This carved tomb was made by a single craftsman, using only an old bayonet as a tool.

▲ These "bis" poles are carved from entire mangrove trees. Figures and exquisitely lacy canopies are carved by the people of New Guinea into the bis poles as fertility symbols.

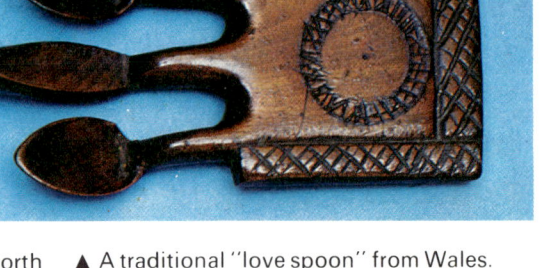

◄ This wood sculpture by Barbara Hepworth has the inviting glossiness and smoothness of texture of a new conker. In this case it is a shame that galleries discourage people from exploring sculpture by touch.

▲ A traditional "love spoon" from Wales. These spoons are made from close-grained woods such as walnut, apple or holly and have geometric designs or lovers' initials or a lover's knot carved on them.

▲ Carved misericord seats are a feature of the choir stalls in medieval churches. They often have unclerical subjects, like this game of football in Gloucester Cathedral.

▼ This painted figurehead is the only remaining relic from the 74-gun sailing ship HMS Ajax built in the late 1700s. Carved out of oak, it represents the mythical hero of the ship's name.

▲ This extraordinary living tree-turret was known as the Maple of Ratibor. The floors of the two sections were made of branches woven together with a natural carpet of leaves.

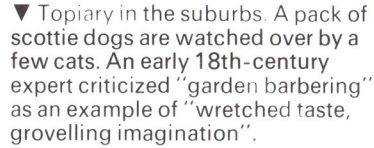

▼ Topiary in the suburbs. A pack of scottie dogs are watched over by a few cats. An early 18th-century expert criticized "garden barbering" as an example of "wretched taste, grovelling imagination".

Trees in the environment

How trees affect the environment

Once upon a time the Sahara desert was a forest. Before the early civilizations of the Greeks and Romans the Mediterranean was not dry and sparse as it is now, but richly covered with trees. More recently settlers in North America cleared vast and beautiful forests—and created the barren "dust bowl". The abuse continues even today.

As early as 1664 the notable champion of trees John Evelyn saw the danger of cutting down trees indiscriminately and wrote a sensible and deeply-felt plea for replanting. It is only comparatively recently however that this has been done on a large scale.

It is not simply their timber value that makes trees important; they play a part in the shape of our environment. Soil beneath trees is made rich with leaf mould. Tree roots hold the soil together, preventing erosion. There is always coolness and moisture in a forest. Even though the sun above may be furiously hot, inside the forest it is damp and fertile. Remove the trees and the land is baked, the soil eroded and washed away, leaving an infertile waste, windblown and liable to flooding.

How the environment affects trees

There are tropical and temperate species of trees, but in general trees don't grow well at very high altitudes or in climates that are excessively dry or cold. Trees growing in such conditions have usually adapted strange ways of dealing with them. There is the dwarf birch, a sprawly little plant which grows up mountains, and the extraordinary bristlecone pines which have been calculated to be 5000 years old! In difficult conditions trees grow more slowly and live longer. This is true of normally fast-growing species; there are records of a sitka spruce which had a hard battle to reach 30 cm in 98 years. By contrast, a balsa grown experimentally in ideal conditions shot up 30 metres in five years.

▶ Wistman's wood (one of the few natural forests in Britain) shows what happens to a forest growing at a high altitude and in poor soil. This oak wood also suffers severe attack from the winter moth. The trees are small and stunted and extremely old. The odd thing is that this wood, thought to be dying, has recently taken a new lease of life and has begun to increase in size.

◀ Tree mountaineers? Some hardy species will survive even quite high up mountainsides if they can find a pocket of soil and adequate shelter. But there is a certain point above which conditions are too poor for growth. This is known as the tree line.

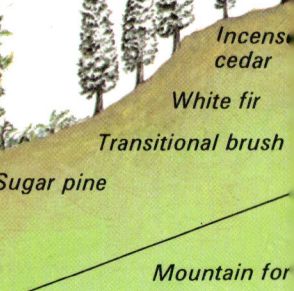

Giant sequoia

Incense cedar

White fir

Transitional brush

Sugar pine

Ponderosa pine

Mountain for

Digger pine

Chaparral

Blue oak

Pine—oak woodland

▲ This eroded hillside in Spain shows the damage that follows when the protective covering of trees is removed. Soil is washed away and deep, barren gullies form where there was once a forest giving shelter to many plants and animals.

▲ Death by pollution. These trees have been killed by one of the most poisonous gases, fluorine, given out from the nearby brickworks. The gas is dissolved by the rain and washed into the soil, where it is taken in by plants.

The trees of one mountain range

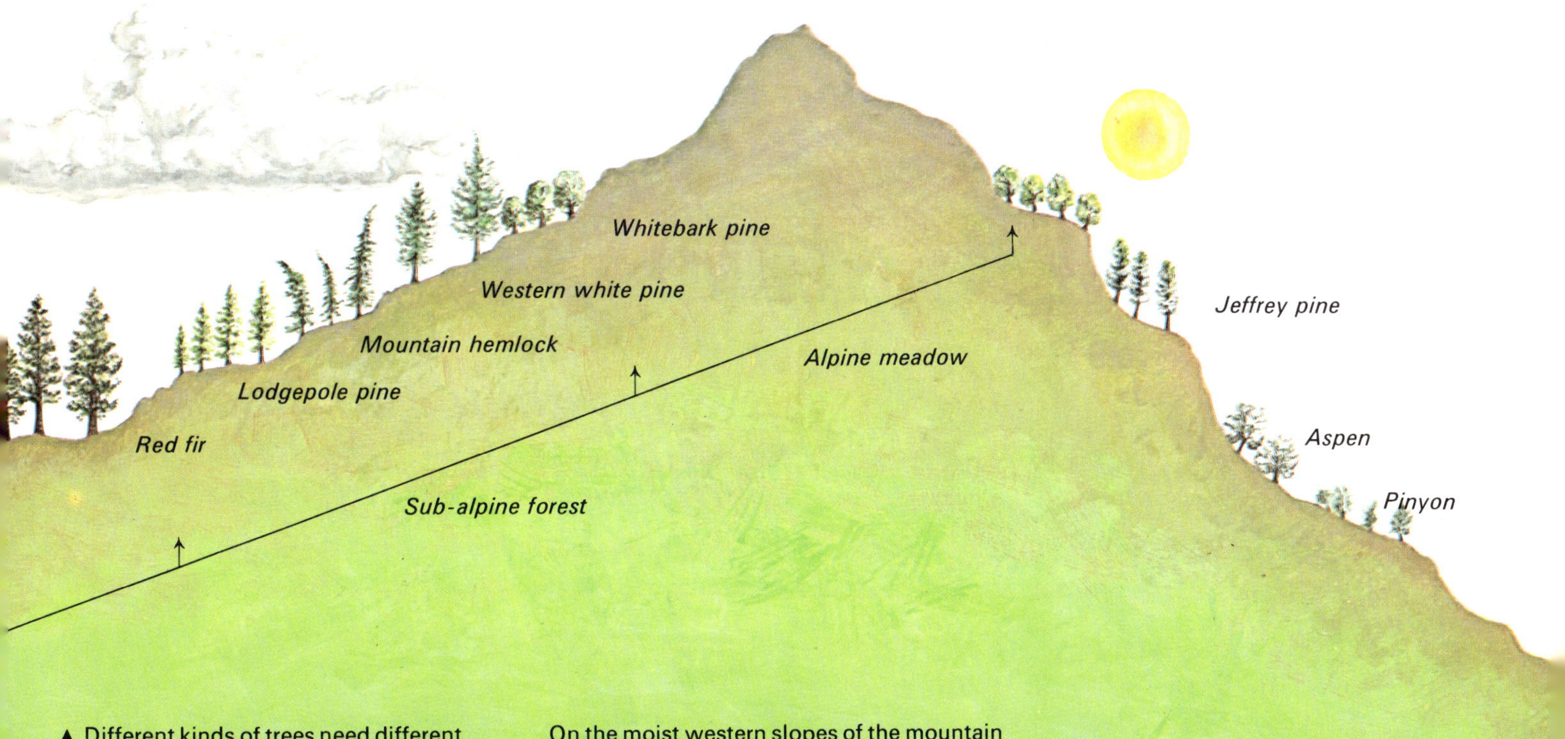

Whitebark pine

Western white pine

Mountain hemlock

Lodgepole pine

Red fir

Sub-alpine forest

Alpine meadow

Jeffrey pine

Aspen

Pinyon

▲ Different kinds of trees need different conditions for growth. Altitude and rainfall are two important factors affecting tree growth. This diagrammatic representation of the Sierra Nevada mountain range in California shows the succession of various types of forest. The wildlife communities supported by these forests also change as the height increases.

On the moist western slopes of the mountain range, the lowest levels support thick pine and oak woodland. This gives way, higher up, to mountain forest of cedar and fir. Still higher in sub-alpine reaches trees are smaller and sparser until the tree line is reached. On the steep, dry eastern side of the mountains only the hardiest species can survive.

Trees and the landscape

▲ This Egyptian painting shows a nobleman's garden, with formally planted trees round a fishpond. Although the trees are fruit trees, they were probably planted for decoration as well.

Trees for pleasure

It is difficult to imagine life without trees. For thousands of years trees have been planted, not only for commercial uses like timber and fruit, but also purely for pleasure. People have always enjoyed looking at trees and walking in their shade.

Planting trees for pleasure is just as much subject to fashion as architecture, painting or dress. In the eighteenth century trees were planted in formal rows and patterns, whereas in the nineteenth century they were informally landscaped. Today trees are planted informally, but on a much smaller scale. They are usually planted to soften the harshness of houses and streets.

It is often difficult to distinguish between trees that have been planted and those that have grown up naturally. Many of the woods that people enjoy today, for example, were carefully planned, although they now look completely natural.

However trees are planted they always add to people's enjoyment whether in a town or in the countryside.

▼ This formal eighteenth-century garden has every tree placed with mathematical precision. The garden reflects the symmetry of the house.

▼ Many roads and driveways are bordered by an avenue of trees of a particular species. France is well known for the poplars which line many of its roads.

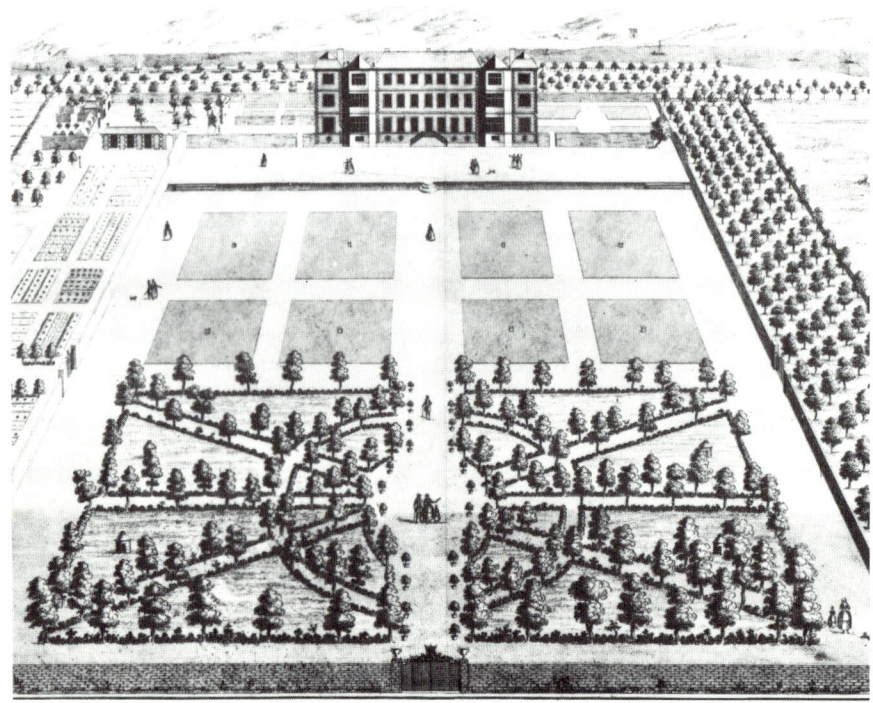

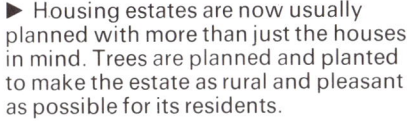

▲ Stourhead in Wiltshire, England is one of the finest examples of a planned, but informal garden. The full beauty of this garden could not have been seen by the people who planted it as the trees only reach maturity after several generations.

▶ Housing estates are now usually planned with more than just the houses in mind. Trees are planned and planted to make the estate as rural and pleasant as possible for its residents.

"Natural" forests

▲ ▶ Many forests and woods were planted several hundred years ago. Some were planted for their wood, but were also used for sports like hunting. Others are preserved like this national park in Japan for the pleasure and enjoyment of everyone.

Projects things to do with trees

Identifying trees

It's not difficult to learn to identify the main species of trees, and it's worth doing for your own pleasure as well as for the purposes of a tree survey. Get hold of a good guide to trees (*A Field Guide to the Trees of Britain and Northern Europe*, by Alan Mitchell published by Collins is the standard one). It will seem confusing at first but just make sure that you have an idea about the main families of trees, don't worry about the many different varieties.

Look up a tree you know as a start, say an oak. You'll find it's got a double name. The common oak is *Quercus robur*. *Quercus* is a family name, like your surname, while *robur* tells you what kind of an oak it is. (You will find the Latin names for the trees mentioned in this book in the index.) You will soon get to know which trees are which without thinking, but to start with you will have to look for the main recognition points: leaf shape, bark, twigs, overall shape, fruits.

It could help you to begin with if you went out with someone who is familiar with trees. Visiting an *arboretum* (a collection of growing trees) can be fun too, because you not only see fine and unusual specimens but can also check your guesses about their names. (There is a list of some of the collections all over the country on page 46.)

Oak

Help needed on tree surveys

In order to get representative results, professional botanists have grown to rely on the help of the general public in natural-history surveys. Individuals, groups and schools are responsible for much of the basic research on major projects. Two long-term projects now under way are the National Tree Survey and the Hedgerow Survey.

National Tree Survey

This project has a double purpose: to record where fine trees are growing which should be conserved and cared for, and to suggest priority areas for tree planting. A leaflet issued by the Tree Council shows how to go about the survey. Write to:
The National Tree Survey
The Tree Council
Room C10/13, 2 Marsham Street
London SW1P 3EP

Hedgerow Survey

The purpose of this survey is to see what trees and shrubs make up our hedges all over the country, to look at the various types and examine what kind of looking after they get. You could find as many as ten or twelve species of trees and shrubs in an old hedge and a great deal of wildlife sheltering within it. Help is particularly needed from the north of England. Write to:
The Hedgerow Survey
Monks Wood Experimental Station
Abbots Ripton, Huntingdonshire

▶ To make a tree survey you need to mark all the trees in your area on a map. Single trees, **T**, should be drawn as a dot with a circle round it. If there is more than one single tree they should be marked **T1**, **T2**, etc. Areas of trees and hedges with too many trees to list singly should be shown by dots, with the code letter **A** and the number of trees. Groups of trees should be shown by **G**. Woods should be outlined and labelled **W**. Name as many of the trees as possible. Mark hedges without trees with a squiggled line and an **H**.

▼ When you have finished the map make a table like the one below giving further details of your survey.

Tree No.	Species	Approx. height	Circumference at base	Comments
T4	Oak	15 m	2.5 m	Beautifully shaped, well known landmark
T5	Horse chestnut	25 m	2.75 m	Much dead wood; poor leafing.
T6	Elm	21 m	2.5 m	Almost dead.
A10	Hazel hedge with ash, oak, yew trees.	12 m max.	1 m av.	Some promising young oaks.
A11	ditto	ditto	ditto	Yews becoming dominant.
G1	Beech	18 m av.	2.5 m	11 mature beeches; 6 of them in poor condition.

Grow your own trees

Instead of throwing away apple and orange pips and avocado, date or peach stones, try planting them. In a few months you could have a fine collection of seedlings. Try oak, pine and horse chestnut too; in fact try everything!.

Avocado

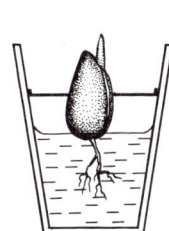

Suspend the stone of an avocado pear in a glass of water, with the stone just touching the water. After three to eight weeks the stone should split and a root and stem emerge. When there are several good roots transfer the stone to a pot of sandy earth. In a warm, sunny spot it will soon grow.

Crack the peach stone gently before putting it 3 cm deep in a pot. In a warm room it will soon start to grow.

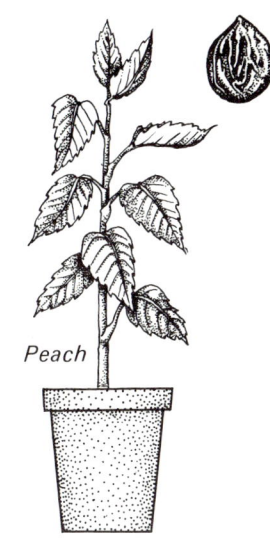

Avocado   *Peach*

The devastating Dutch elm disease

WATCH for the first signs of disease. Your observation could save a tree's life so get together with a few friends to monitor all the elms in your area.
The first signs of disease are: *autumn in summer,* a patchy yellowing of clumps of foliage. In winter you will notice the little *shepherd's crooks* of the twigs which curl downwards as they die.

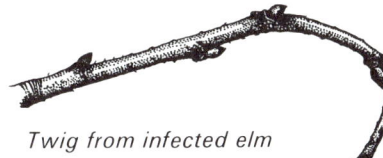

Elm   *Twig from infected elm*

Once you have identified a diseased tree, prompt action is essential.
The effects of Dutch elm disease are widespread and devastating. No certain cure has yet been found but the injection of fungicide into the trunk at the first sign of disease gives the tree about twice the chance of survival. To have this treatment done commercially is expensive, but with access to the equipment small groups of people can in a short while learn how to do it for themselves—at a fraction of the cost.
   Form an "elm watch" group.
   Put pressure on your local natural history society conservation group, and local authority to *do* something before it is too late.
   Plant and tend new trees. It will take a long time to replace all the beautiful old trees that have died so make a start now.

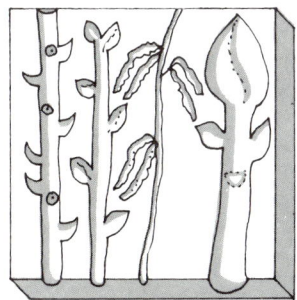

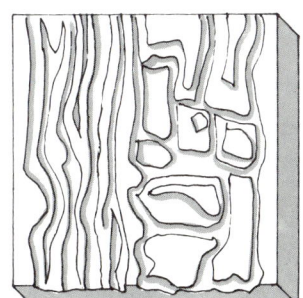

Making and printing

Decorative tiles
Make some dough from two cups of flour, one cup of salt and one cup of water. Knead the mixture well and roll it out with a rolling pin until it is about 15 mm thick. Trim the dough into a square tile. Press bark, seeds or twigs onto the tile to make a pattern. When the pattern is finished dry the tile in a warm place. The dry tile can be painted or varnished.

Printed wood
Visit a timber yard and find out all the shapes that wood is cut into. There are special shapes for skirting boards, round door frames, etc. Get some of the more interesting shapes to make printed patterns. Smooth the surface of the wood you are going to use for printing with glass paper. Print using paint or printing ink on paper that is placed on a pad of newspaper (the soft base will help to get a good impression). Or use a cold dye and print onto cloth following the instructions on the packet.

Reference find out more about trees

Glossary

cambium   a thin sheath of growth cells just inside the bark. If it is damaged the tree will die.

chlorophyll   a substance in all green plants used in photosynthesis.

cotyledons   the seed leaves of a tree.

deciduous   trees which shed their leaves in autumn.

evergreen   trees which do not shed their leaves in winter. As they lose their old leaves, they grow new ones so their branches are never bare.

fossil   petrified remains of a plant or animal from prehistoric times. Tree fossils have usually been compressed by the pressure of the earth into materials like coal.

hardwood   wood from broadleaf trees, grained wood usually used to make furniture.

heartwood   the dead wood in the trunk, which acts as the tree's support.

phloem   outer layer of cells just inside the bark, through which the sap passes from the leaves to the rest of the tree.

photosynthesis   the way in which trees and other green plants make their food.

softwood   wood from coniferous trees, its most important use is in paper-making.

transpiration   the process by which water is let out into the atmosphere from the tree's leaves.

vascular bundles   bundles of veins made up of phloem and xylem which link the living parts of the tree.

xylem   inner layer of cells just inside the bark, which carry water and minerals up from the roots to the rest of the tree.

Places to visit

This very short list of gardens with unusual and interesting trees is only a rough guide. All over the country there are gardens and parks which are always worth a visit. You will find many more places of interest included at the end of most books about trees.

Tresco Abbey
Isles of Scilly
Has an extraordinary collection of Southern Hemisphere trees.

Westonbirt Arboretum
Near Tetbury
Gloucestershire
A 50-hectare landscaped planting of immense variety. Nearby is Silk Wood, 2km walk away, which is lined both sides all the way with rare trees and bays of collections.

Royal Botanic Gardens
Kew
Surrey
The largest specimens of numerous of the rarest species; unequalled collections of most genera, notably oaks, celtises, limes, zelkovas, catalpas.

Studley Royal and Fountains Abbey
Near Ripon
Yorkshire
They have many big trees; notably sweet chestnut, oaks.

Vivod Forest Garden
above Vivod House
near Llangollen
Clwyd
A young arboretum of many rare species; forest plots covering a wide range.

Dawyck
Stobo
Peebleshire
An extensive collection of conifers, maples, and many rare trees. Original Dawyck Beech, very early larch, Douglas fir, western hemlock, fine Asiatic silver firs.

Glasnevin Botanic Garden
Dublin
A large collection with many fine, very rare trees.

Suggested booklist

The International Book of Trees by Hugh Johnson (Mitchell Beazley). Splendid full-colour guide. As good to read as to look at.

Know your Broadleaves; Know your Conifers both by H L Edlin (H.M.S.O.). Good value Forestry Commission books. Many other leaflets on trees and forests available, including *The Biology of Dutch Elm Disease* which tells you all about it—or as much as we know.

Trees in the Wild by Gerald Wilkinson (Hope). Very readable survey of woodland trees.

Conifers and Allies; Broadleaved Trees Book 1 (Jarrold). Two good inexpensive little books with colour photographs.

Woodland by William Condry (Collins). A survey of forests and forest life.

Trees in History and Legend by J H Wilkes (Muller).

The World of a Tree by A Darlington (Faber). Fascinating account of the life an oak-tree supports.

What tree is that? Miles Hadfield (Faber). Good first identification book with interesting notes.

A Field Guide to the Trees of Britain and Northern Europe by A Mitchell (Collins). Most comprehensive identification book around.

Tree Preservation Orders

Anyone can apply for a preservation order for any tree. Building contractors have to get permission to cut down trees, but often don't bother. Keep an eye on them. If you know of a fine tree which you think should be protected, or you see some trees in danger, write to your local authority about it. Trees take a long time to grow; once felled they can't be put back in a hurry. Your action could save a tree; it's worth keeping an alert eye and a pen at the ready.

Index

Illustration Credits
Key to the positions of illustrations: (T) top, (C) centre,
(B) bottom, and combinations; for example (TR) top
right, or (CL) centre left.

Artists
Allard Design Group Ltd 20-21
Peter Connolly 29, 31
Ron Hayward Associates 4-5, 19
Gillian Lockwood 45 (B)
Vanessa Luff 6-7, 8-9, 14-15, 26, 36-37, 40-41, 44,
 45 (T) (C)
Tony Morris 24
Tony Payne 22, 28
Gary Rees 10-11, 12-13, 16
Colin Smithson 42-3

Photographs and Prints
A-Z Collection 3 (TR) (C) (BL) (BR), 7 (B), 15 (BL),
 19 (BL), 23 (BR), 32 (TR), 33 (TL)
Michael Abrahams 33 (BL)
Heather Angel 7 (T) (C), 13 (T) (C), 17 (T), 18 (BL)
 (BR), 22 (BR), 23 (C) (BL), 36 (CB) (B), 37 (B)
 (CB) (CT) (T), 41 (TL)
Ardea Photographics 41 (TR)
Associated Press 30 (BL)
Herbert G Baker 22 (TR)
S C Bisserot 40 (TR)
British Museum (Natural History) 5 (BR)
The Brooklyn Museum 34 (BL)
Civic Trees Ltd 33 (TR) (C) (BR)

Courtaulds Ltd 21 (TL) (TR)
D N Dalton (NHPA) 19 (BR)
Geoffrey Drury 26 (TL) (BR)
Bob Edwards 30 (T) (C)
Ted Ellis 36 (T) (CT)
Enso Marketing 21 (BR)
Robert Estall 19 (CR)
Forestry Commission 6, 23 (TL) (TR), 27 (T) (C) (B),
 30 (BR), 32 (BL)
Mr L Harris 9 (CL)
F N Hepper 17 (BR)
John Hillelson Agency Ltd 39 (BR)
Ikon 34 (TR), 39 (TL)
Keystone Press 32 (BR)
John Lawrence 21 (BL)
Claire Leimbach 17 (BL), 38 (TR), 40 (BL)
Mansell Collection 9 (BL) (BR)
Mary Evans Picture Library 35 (CR) (B), 39 (TR)
Michael Holford Library 25 (T) (CL), 35 (TR)
National Maritime Museum 39 (BL)
Maurice Nimmo 8
I Polunin (NHPA) 16
George Rainbird 18 (T) (C)
Reed Paper and Board UK (Ltd) 20 (TR) (BL) (BR)
Spectrum 15 (BR)
James Tallon (NHPA) 5 (BL)
Tate Gallery 38 (BL)
The Welsh Folk Museum 38 (BR)
Woodmansterne 9 (CR)

proost Turnhout (Belgium)

PRINTED IN BELGIUM